An Exposition of the
On the Hebdomads
of Boethius

✤o✤

THOMAS AQUINAS IN TRANSLATION

ST. THOMAS AQUINAS

An Exposition of the *On the Hebdomads* of Boethius

[*Expositio libri Boetii De ebdomadibus*]

Introduction and translation by

Janice L. Schultz and

†Edward A. Synan

The Catholic University of America Press
Washington, D.C.

The paper used in this publication meets the minimum requirements of
American National Standards for Information Science—Permanence of Paper
for Printed Library materials, ANSI Z39.48-1984.

∞

Library of Congress Cataloging-in-Publication Data

Thomas, Aquinas, Saint, 1225?–1274
    [Expositio in librum Boethii De hebdomadibus. English]
    An exposition of the On the hebdomads of Boethius / St. Thomas
Aquinas ; introduction and translation by Janice L. Schultz and
Edward A. Synan.
      p. cm—(Thomas Aquinas in translation)
    Includes bibliographical references and index.
    ISBN 0-8132-0994-3 (alk. paper) — ISBN 0-8132-0995-1 (pbk. :
alk. paper)
      1. Boethius, d. 524. Quomodo substantiae. I. Schultz, Janice L.,
1945– II. Synan, Edward A. III. Boethius, d. 524. Quomodo
substantiae. English. IV. Title. V. Series.
    PA6231.Q7 T48   2001
    189—dc21

                                 00-037883

To Louis J. Bataillon and to the memory of
Carlo A. Grassi, Leonine editors of this work.

While this manuscript was under review, Edward A. Synan passed away after a short illness. When I explained to a colleague of his that Msgr. Synan had had a weak heart since 1959, the reply captured the feelings of so many: "If Fr. Synan's heart was weak, it was only in the narrowest biological sense!" Those who knew Edward Synan loved him, but whether or not he realized this, he embraced all he met with a profound spirit of *amor amicitiae*, love of friendship, as integral to his Christian way of living. To have known him was a singular blessing; to have worked with him, an enormous privilege and delight. And so whatever may be of value in my portion of this manuscript I dedicate in a special way to the memory of Edward A. Synan: most kind and generous teacher and mentor, adopted family member, dearest of friends.

—J.L.S

CONTENTS

ACKNOWLEDGMENTS

Deep gratitude is here expressed for the permission of the Leonine editors to include with our translation the Latin text they have established, conveyed to us in a letter from Louis J. Bataillon; their kindness is greatly appreciated.

Edward A. Synan and Janice L. Schultz
May 1997

Sincere thanks is extended to Paul V. Spade, Professor of Philosophy at Indiana University who, after Msgr. Synan's passing, reviewed difficult passages and made most helpful suggestions for the final manuscript. I wish also to thank Professor Kevin White of The Catholic University of America for his careful final reading and remarks, and my family and friends for their help and encouragement, especially my husband, Len, and my parents; Mary Jane Gormley, Dana Cushing, and Rev. James K. Farge, C.S.B., Senior Fellow at the Pontifical Institute of Mediaeval Studies in Toronto. Finally, I am very grateful to Canisius College for a summer grant that helped support my research.

Janice L. Schultz
November 1999

INTRODUCTION

These introductory remarks are intended to assist a modern reader in understanding two difficult works by two difficult authors. Those works are a short treatise by Anicius Manlius Severinus Boethius (ca. 480–524), a work known to the Middle Ages as *On the Hebdomads* (the meaning of this very title will require discussion), and an exposition of that treatise by Thomas Aquinas (ca. 1225–1274). Both are presented here in our English translation of the "Leonine edition" text of 1992, tome 50, of the *Opera omnia* of Saint Thomas, for that edition proffers the words of Boethius along with the explanations by Brother Thomas. Intrinsic difficulties of these two works are compounded by academic and cultural transformations; the world of Boethius was not the world of Aquinas and our world is identical with neither of the two worlds that produced those authors. We have been reminded by Armand Maurer that seven centuries separate Boethius and Thomas Aquinas;[1] it is also true that seven centuries separate us from Aquinas. Difficulties arising from these temporal separations are aggravated in a paradoxical way by the fact that both authors are esteemed especially in the "scholastic" tradition; the more one has been formed in some stream of that tradition (for it is far from monolithic) the more difficult becomes an objective reading of either author. Quite apart from the tradition of scholastic philosophy, other movements tend to cloud our modern vision. Approaches modish in the last fifty years—existentialism, logical positivism, phenomenology, to say nothing of advances in the understanding of the Thomistic analysis of beings, *encia,* under the sign of "potency" and "act," in Thomistic terms *essencia* and *esse*—all these are capable of distorting one's interpretation of Boethian terms. In this double work, an exposition by Saint Thomas Aquinas of a writing by Boethius, the last Roman used the term *esse* frequently; the Angelic Doctor often employed, in addition, the allied terms *essencia* and *ens.* Contrasted with

1. *Thomas Aquinas. Faith, reason and theology,* tr. Armand Maurer, Mediaeval Sources in Translation 32 (Toronto: 1987), p. xxxv.

the Boethian *esse* is the Boethian *quod est* or *id quod est;* the interpretation of all these technical terms, particularly *esse*, presents difficulty.

The Background

Biographical and bibliographical data on these authors will be provided only to the point that seems helpful in understanding the works presented. For the first, it must be recalled that the works of Boethius enjoyed a significant afterlife well into the eighteenth century, thanks to his enormous prestige with the literate public. Edward Gibbon, for instance, in an often-quoted line, termed *The Consolation of Philosophy* by Boethius "a golden volume, not unworthy of the leisure of Plato or Tully,"[2] and in the same chapter Gibbon remarked that "the senator Boethius is the last of the Romans whom Cato or Tully could have acknowledged for their countryman."[3] As Professor Henry Chadwick has noted, this second remark of Gibbon's echoes Lorenzo Valla: For that renaissance scholar, Boethius was "the last of the erudite."[4] Aquinas, who has provided the explanation of the treatise by Boethius, shares with Augustine of Hippo (354–430) intellectual preeminence in the history of Christian thought.

During the waning years of the imperial Roman tradition, Boethius had been given an education in both Latin and Greek. Although bilingualism was still held to be suitable for the old aristocracy, Boethius seems to have impressed his contemporaries as exceptional in his control of the Greek language as well as in his control of Greek science and philosophy. Through him, it was said, not without hyperbole:

> Thanks to your translations, Pythagoras, master of music, Ptolomeus, the astronomer, are read as if they were natives of Italy; Nicomachus, the

2. Edward Gibbon, *The History of the Decline and Fall of the Roman Empire*, ed. J.B. Bury (London: 1909), vol. 4, ch. 39, p. 215.

3. Ibidem, pp. 211.

4. Henry Chadwick, *Boethius. The Consolations of Music, Logic, Theology, and Philosophy*, Oxford: 1981 (hereafter Chadwick), p. xi; Valla's remark in which Professor Chadwick has seen the source of Gibbon's celebrated comment was " . . . eruditorum vltimus Boetius . . ."; see *Lavrentii Vallae opera . . .* (Basel: 1540), vol.1, p. 644 (rpt., Turin: E. Garin, 1962). For a discussion of all parties (Boethius, Valla, Gibbon, and Chadwick), see "Boethius, Valla, and Gibbon" by Edward A. Synan in *The Modern Schoolman* 69.3 & 4, (March/May 1992), pp. 475–91, a *Festschrift* edition of the journal for Professor Vernon J. Bourke.

arithmetician, Euclid, the geometrician, are heard as if they were natives of Ausonia [a literary term for Italy]; Plato, master of the divine *(theologus)* Aristotle, master of logic, debate in the speech of Romulus; the master of mechanics too, Archimedes, you have rendered a native of Latium for the sake of Sicilians . . .[5]

If not so extensive as the rhetoric of Cassiodorus would have us believe, the collection of translations, as well as of original works on certain of the seven liberal arts, which Boethius has bequeathed to his successors, is indeed extensive. The very term *quadrivium* to name the four mathematical arts is owing to his conception of them as the "fourfold path" to wisdom,[6] a designation matched by an unknown successor who, in the same spirit, named the three verbal arts the *trivium,* the "threefold path" to wisdom. A most significant part of the mediaeval acquaintance with classical thought, especially in "dialectic," was due to the labors of Boethius. His translations of the *Categories* and the *On Interpretation* of Aristotle, along with his commentaries on them, were essential elements of the "old logic." The two translations conveyed Aristotle to the west until the mid-twelfth century. Boethius's original essays on dialectic and rhetoric, to say nothing of his extremely influential commentaries on the *Isagoge* of Porphyry,[7] represented "Aristotelianism," if not Aristotle, to the Latin-speaking world. All this was expanded by a block of essays that in our day are known, anachronistically, as the "theological tractates." This use of "theological" for an early-sixth-century writing is anachronistic since the term "theology" to designate the scientific exploration of religious faith as distinguished from credally neutral "philosophy" was introduced, and not without difficulty, only in the twelfth century. This innovation was counted as one more outrage of its author, Peter Abelard. The Senator Cassiodorus, a contemporary and correspon-

5. "Translationibus enim tuis Pythagoras musicus, Ptolemaeus astronomus leguntur Itali: Nicomachus arithmeticus, geometricus Euclides audiuntur Ausonii: Plato theologus, Aristoteles logicus Quirinali voce disceptant: mechanicum etiam Archimedem Latialem Siculis reddidisti . . . ," Cassiodorus, *Variarum* 1.45; MGH AA 12, p. 40, ll. 11–15.

6. ". . . haud quemqam in philosophiae disciplinis ad cumulum perfectionis evadere, nisi cui talis prudentiae nobilitas quodam quasi quadrivio vestigatur . . . ," *De arithmetica* 1.1; PL 63 1079.

7. For the best edition see that by G. Schepss and S. Brandt, CSEL 48 (Vienna and Leipzig: 1906).

dent of Boethius, as shown by the well-known *Ordo generis,* a fragment discovered by Alfred Holder and published in 1877 by Hermann Usener, had named those essays more suitably "dogmatic chapters." *On the Hebdomads (De hebdomadibus),* our present concern, is the third of those "chapters."

Two predecessors exercised an effective and demonstrable influence on the thought and expression of Boethius, but in quite different ways. The first of these was Marcus Tullius Cicero (106–43 b.c.). Even in externals the careers of Cicero and Boethius manifest striking parallels, including the deaths of both owing to political turmoil.

Cicero

Both Cicero and Boethius combined an interest in letters with political activity. So too were their respective moments in history similar. Cicero lived during the decades when the polity of Rome was shifting from a republic to an empire, Boethius at a time when an Ostrogothic King ruled Italy, but with the old imperial civil service still in place, a service in which Boethius himself, his sons, and his father-in-law held high office. As Cicero had been Consul in 63 b.c., so Boethius held that office in a.d. 510; in 522 the two sons of Boethius, despite their extreme youth, jointly held the same office. Their nomination Boethius counted the highpoint of his life; at the end of his career Boethius was Master of Offices. These two scholars, Cicero and Boethius, paid with their lives for their political activities. Cicero was "proscribed" and executed by the triumvirate, Boethius executed on trumped-up charges of high treason and sorcery by the Ostrogothic King, Theodoric. Intellectual parallels are no less striking.

Cicero had been persuaded that to bring Greek philosophical thought within the reach of Romans, both by translating Greek philosophical works into Latin and by original compositions, was a worthy occupation for a public figure at leisure. Cicero felt that government was a suitable theme for properly philosophical treatment and that this had been the view of the greatest among the philosophers, for it had been "most elaborately treated by Plato, Aristotle, Theophrastus, and the entire Peripatetic school,"[8] to say nothing of himself, author of a treatise *On the*

---

8. "Magnus locus philosophiaeque proprius a Platone, Aristotele, Theophrasto totaque Peripateticorum familia tractatus uberrime." *De divinatione* 2.1.3.

Commonwealth. Citing a title of which Boethius cannot have been unaware, Cicero went on: "What need is there to say anything of my treatise *On Consolation?* For it is the source of very great comfort to me and
will, I think, be of much help to others."[9] Cicero's public duties had
blocked a philosophical project:

> . . . if some most grievous cause had not intervened there would not now
> be any phase of philosophy which I had failed to elucidate and make eas-
> ily accessible in the Latin tongue. For what greater or better service can I
> render to the commonwealth than to instruct and train the youth . . . ?
> . . . it would redound to the fame and glory of the Roman people to be
> made independent of Greek writers in the study of philosophy, and this
> result I shall certainly bring about if my present plans are accomplished.[10]

Nor was Cicero blind to the gratitude he might expect from this contri-
bution to Roman culture: ". . . my countrymen will pardon me—rather
they will thank me . . ."[11] Remarks to this effect are all but duplicated by
well-known passages in Boethius:

> If the cares of the Consul's office prevent our devoting all our leisure and
> energy to these studies, it nonetheless seems to be a part of concern for
> the commonwealth to instruct her citizens . . . Nor should I merit ill of
> my fellow citizens if, since virtue of old consisted in transferring the gov-
> ernance and rule of foreign cities to this single commonwealth, I at least
> do what is left: imbue the doings of our state with the arts of Greek wis-
> dom. Hence this is by no means alien to the office of Consul . . .[12]

9. "Nam quid ego *de Consolatione* dicam? quae mihi quidem ipsi sane aliquan-
tum medetur, ceteris item multum illam profuturam puto." Ibidem.
    10. ". . . nisi quae causa gravior obstitisset, nullum philosophiae locum esse
pateremur, qui non Latinis litteris illustratus pateret. Quod enim munus rei pub-
licae afferre maius meliusve possumus, quam si docemus atque erudimus iuven-
tutem, . . . Magnificum illud etiam Romanisque hominibus gloriosum, ut Graecis
de philosophia litteris non egeant; quod adsequar profecto, si instituta perfe-
cero." Ibidem 2.2.4–6. This was not an isolated remark of Cicero on the "public"
value of philosophical translation by a statesman: "Ego vero, quoniam forensibus
operis, laboribus, periculis non deseruisse mihi videor praesidium in quo a popu-
lo Romano locatus sum, debeo profecto, quantumcumque possum, in eo quoque
elaborare ut sint opera, studio, labore meo doctiores cives mei . . . ," *De finibus*
1.4.10.
    11. "Dabunt igitur mihi veniam mei cives vel gratiam potius habebunt . . . ,"
De divinatione 2.2.6.
    12. "Et si nos curae officii consularis impediunt quo minus in his studiis

Boethius proposed to effect this in the way that Cicero had intended, by translations and by commentaries:

> I was writing away, turning into Roman style every work whatever of Aristotle that fell into my hands as well as writing commentaries on them in the Latin tongue . . . So too, by translating all the Dialogues of Plato and commenting on them, I would render this also in Latin form.[13]

Boethius followed these lines with what has always been seen correctly as evidence of his "Neoplatonic" conviction that, in the end and despite surface differences, the philosophy of Aristotle and that of Plato are identical:

> In doing these things I would by no means despise the project of recalling the opinions proper to Aristotle and Plato to a kind of single harmony and of showing that they are not (as so many think) at odds on everything, but that on most points in philosophy they are very much in agreement. If life and leisure be granted, I should like to make this effort, both for the sake of the considerable value of the project, and also for the acclaim that ought to greet it, at least on the part of those whom envy does not sour.[14]

Although Cicero had not explicitly made Platonic and Aristotelian philosophy a single block of thought, he had associated the two philosophers[15] with even-handed praise for both. Here it will not be out of

---

omne otium plenamque operam consumimus, pertinere tamen videtur hoc ad aliquam reipublicae curam, elucubratae rei doctrina cives instruere. Nec male de civibus meis merear, si cum prisca hominum virtus urbium caeterarum ad hanc unam rempublicam, dominationem, imperiumque transtulerit, ego id saltem quod reliquum est, Graecae sapientiae artibus mores nostrae civitatis instruxero. Quare ne hoc quidem ipsum consulis vacat officio . . . ," *In Categorias Aristotelis* 2; PL 64 201B.

13. "Ego omne Aristotelis opus quodcunque in manus venerit, in Romanum stylum vertens, eorum omnium commenta Latina oratione perscribam, . . . omnesque Platonis dialogos vertendo, vel etiam commentando in Latinam redigam formam." *Liber De interpretatione*, ed. secunda, 2; PL 64 433.

14. "His peractis non equidem contempserim Aristotelis Platonisque sententias, in unam quodammodo revocare concordiam, et in his eos non ut plerique dissentire in omnibus, sed in plerisque quae sunt in philosophia maxime consentire demonstrem, haec si vita otiumque superit, cum multa operis hujus utilitate, nec non etiam laude contenderim, qua in re faveant oportet, quos nulla coquit invidia." Ibidem.

15. "Quamquam si plane sic verterem Platonem aut Aristotelem . . . eorum

place to remark that Plato and Aristotle, despite their dissent on where the abstract and universal "form" ought to be located, were at one in asserting that philosophy deals exclusively with that form. Neither one justified a scientific approach to the existent singular of experience: The Platonic "Form" and the Aristotelian "universal" they counted the sole objects of scientific knowledge. Indeed, the middle ages would produce a considerable literature on how theology might be, in fact, "scientific" despite its concern with concrete singulars. Both Augustine and Boethius, we shall argue, reflect this philosophical focus on the universal, essential, form.

An important bit of evidence on the esteem Boethius entertained for Cicero is that he wrote a commentary on Cicero's *Topics*. It may be noted also that Cicero's preoccupation with the problem posed to a pagan by "fate" and human freedom (he wrote a work *On Fate*, for instance) was matched by the biblically acceptable conception proposed by Boethius in his *Consolation of Philosophy*, Book 5.[16] The laws of nature, the "fate" of the pagans, like the free choices by humans, are all subject to divine Providence.

Augustine

If Cicero seemed to Boethius a suitable model in his double career as scholar and statesman, Augustine he acknowledged, and by name, as the one whose "sowing" he aspired to bring to harvest. Thus Boethius concluded the long dedication of his first "dogmatic chapter," *On the Trinity (De trinitate)*, to his father-in-law, the Senator Quintus Aurelius

---

cognitionem divina illa ingenia transferrem." *De finibus* 1.3.7; ". . . semperque habuit in ore Platonem, Aristotelem, Xenocratem, Theophrastum, Dicaearchum . . . ," ibidem 4.28.79; ". . . Peripatetici veteres, quorum princeps Aristoteles, quem excepto Platone haud scio an recte dixerim principem philosophorum." ibidem 5.3.7; ". . . nata est sententia veterum Academicorum et Peripateticorum ut finem bonorum dicerent secundum naturam vivere . . . ," ibidem 2.11.34; ". . . veteres illos Platonis auditores, Speusippum, Aristotelem, Xenocratem, deinde eorum Polemonem, Theophrastum, satis et copiose et eleganter habuisse constitutam disciplinam . . . ," ibidem 4.2.3.

16. See his discrimination between biblical Providence and the natural order designated as "fate": *Consolatio philosophiae* (*The Consolation of Philosophy*, hereafter *Con.*, in *The Theological Tractates. The Consolation of Philosophy*, tr. H.F. Stewart, E.K. Rand, S.J. Tester [Cambridge and London: Harvard University Press, new ed. 1973; rpt. 1990, The Loeb Classical Library]) 4, pr. 6.

Memmius Symmachus, with an invitation that is also a pledge of allegiance to the Bishop of Hippo: "You must however examine whether the seeds sown in my mind by St. Augustine's writings have borne fruit."[17] Senator Symmachus, father-in-law of Boethius and a conspicuous Christian, was to die a year or so after the execution of Boethius for his alleged part in the same conspiracy that destroyed Boethius. By a historical oddity this Symmachus was a direct descendant of that earlier Senator of the same name who had opposed Ambrose, Bishop of Milan, on the restoration of the altar and statue of the goddess of Victory in the Senate House at Rome. Having lost that battle as leader of the pagan party in the Senate, the older pagan Symmachus had then presided as Prefect of the City over the assignment of the brilliant young Manichee, Aurelius Augustinus, to the post as teacher of rhetoric in the municipal school at Milan and as public orator for special events.[18] There he might have been expected to rival Ambrose, a preacher of reputation. In the event, Symmachus unwittingly provided Ambrose with another, and ultimately more substantive, triumph. Augustine, having read Cicero for the content of his thought rather than, as was fashionable, for his style,[19] went to hear Bishop Ambrose preach for the opposite reason: "not as a teacher of truth," but to evaluate his reputation for eloquence.[20] The preaching of Ambrose, marked by Neoplatonic echoes,[21]

---

17. "Vobis tamen etiam illud inspiciendum est, an ex beati Augustini scriptis semina rationum aliquos in nos uenientia fructus extulerint." *De trinitate* (hereafter *De trin.*, in *The Theological Tractates*, Stewart, Rand, and Tester), proemium, ll. 31–35.

18. "Itaque posteaquam missum est a Mediolanio Romam ad praefectum urbis, ut illi ciuitati rhetoricae magister prouideretur impertita etiam euectione publica, ego ipse ambiui per eos ipsos manichaeis uanitatibus ebrios—quibus ut carerem ibam, sed utrique nesciebamus—ut dictione proposita me probatum praefectus tunc Symmachus mitteret. Et ueni Mediolanium ad Ambrosium episcopum . . . ," Augustine, *Confessionum* 5.13.23, ed. M. Skutella, L. Verheijen, CCSL 27 (Turnhout: 1981), p. 70, ll. 1–7.

19. ". . . perueneram in librum cuiusdam Ciceronis, cuius linguam fere omnes mirantur, pectus non ita. Sed liber ille ipsius exhortationem continet ad philosophiam et uocatur Hortensius. Ille uero liber mutauit affectum meum et ad te ipsum, domine, mutauit preces meas et uota ac desideria mea fecit alia. Viluit mihi repente omnis uana spes et immortalitatem sapientiae concupiscebam aestu cordis incredibili . . . ," *Confessionum* 3.4.7; ed. cit., p. 30, ll. 4–10.

20. "Cum enim non satagerem discere quae dicebat, sed tantum quemadmodum dicebat audire . . . ," *Confessionum* 5.14.24; ed. cit., p. 71, ll. 1, 2.

resolved Augustine's philosophical doubts. It now seemed possible for
him to accept a reality that is not material and to read scriptural language in a nonliteral way.[22] Augustine entered on a catechumenate that
included a "Ciceronian"[23] interlude of philosophical conversations at the
villa of a friend where he resolved his intellectual difficulties. Ultimately
Augustine was baptized by Ambrose himself.[24] As one who was sure he
would find Plato compatible with Christ,[25] Augustine held with
Neoplatonic philosophers that Plato and Aristotle

> . . . sing in unison with each other in such wise that, although to the in-
> experienced and to the less attentive they may seem to disagree—and
> that throughout many a century and many a controversy—one altogeth-
> er true philosophical discipline, as I see it, has been rendered quite evi-
> dent.[26]

On this, it has been seen, Boethius was to agree. It is true that Augustine
gives small evidence of having read much of Aristotle directly (he mentioned in the Confessions 4.16.28 that "alone" he had read and under-

21. See the magistral study by P. Courcelle, Recherches sur les "Confessions" de S.
Augustin (Paris: 1950).

22. Confessionum 5.14.24; ed. cit., p. 71.

23. See parallels observed by Edmund Taite Silk between Cicero's villa dia-
logues and those of Augustine at Cassiciacum, as well as the same scholar's in-
genious suggestion that as Cicero's Hortensius stood to Augustine so the latter's
Cassiciacum dialogues stood to the work of Boethius: "Boethius's Consolatio
Philosophiae as a Sequel to Augustine's Dialogues and Soliloquia," Harvard
Theological Review 32.1 (1939) pp. 19–39.

24. Confessionum 9.6.14; ed. cit., pp. 140, 141.

25. See his remarks at Cassiciacum, Against the Skeptics (Contra Academicos)
3.20.43: "I am confident that among the Platonists I shall find what is not opposed to the teachings of our religion (. . . apud Platonicos me interim, quod sac-
ris nostris non repugnet, reperturum esse confido)." Ed. W.M. Green, CCSL 29
(Turnhout: 1970), p. 61, ll. 23, 24. See A.C. Pegis, "The Mind of St. Augustine,"
Mediaeval Studies 6 (1944) pp. 1–61; the text cited is examined, p. 3, in this semi-
nal article.

26. ". . . Aristotelem ac Platonem ita sibi concinere, ut imperitis minusque at-
tentis dissentire uideantur, multis quidem saeculis multisque contentionibus, sed
tamen eliquata est, ut opinor, una uerissimae philosophiae disciplina." Ibidem
3.19.42; candor compels the admission that the author's affirmative argument,
based on this passage (Edward A. Synan, "An Augustinian Testimony to
Polyphonic Music?" Musica disciplina 18 [1964], pp. 3–6) seems not to have con-
vinced historians of music; that contention is irrelevant to the present issue.

stood the *Categories*). Nor did allegiance to Augustine on the part of Boethius entail the rejection of Cicero, for Augustine too had held Cicero in high regard. Apart from Augustine's repeated references to having read the *Hortensius* at 18 and from that reading to have come to "love wisdom,"[27] much of what can now be reconstructed of that lost dialogue by Cicero is owing to Augustine's 11 citations of the *Hortensius* in six of his own works.[28] In another mood, the young Augustine had admired the "stateliness of Tully";[29] this had been a serious obstacle to his acceptance of the Latin Bible. Two philosophical positions of Augustine seem to be crucial for understanding the *On the Hebdomads* of Boethius.

Augustine on Being. The first of those positions is Augustinian thought and vocabulary on "being," particularly as this mysterious term is said of God. This is a point, and undoubtedly the most important point, on which Augustine found Plato and Scripture in harmony. As he put it in the *Confessions:*

> And I examined those others beneath You and I saw that they neither are altogether, nor are they not altogether; they are, indeed, because they are from You; they are not, because they are not what You are. For this it is that truly is: what remains immutably.[30]

No reader of *Timaeus* 27D will fail to recognize that this echoes Plato's question: "What is it that always is and has no becoming? What is it that is always becoming and never is?" A scriptural passage seemed to Augustine to say nothing else:

> . . . In comparison to that which truly is, because He is immutably, those mutable things, that have been made, are not. Plato held this very

27. *Confessionum* 3.4.7 and 6.11.18; ed. cit., pp. 30, 86.

28. See the edition of the extant fragments of the *Hortensius* in *M.Tullii Ciceronis opera quae supersunt omnia,* ed. J.G. Baiter and C.L. Kayser (Leipzig: 1869), vol. 11, pp. 59–67; the influence of Cicero on our two authors has been mentioned above, note 23.

29. ". . . illam scripturam . . . uisa est mihi indigna, quam Tullianae dignitati compararem." *Confessionum* 3.5.9; ed. cit., p. 31, ll. 6, 7.

30. "Et inspexi cetera infra te et uidi nec omnino esse nec omnino non esse: esse quidem, quoniam abs te sunt, non esse autem, quoniam id quod es non sunt. Id enim uere est, quod incommutabiliter manet." *Confessionum* 7.11.17; ed. cit., p. 104, ll. 1–4.

strongly and insisted upon it most carefully. I do not know whether it is to be found in the books of those who were before Plato, except where it is said: "I am . . ." [Exodus 3:14].[31]

All this is reinforced by a passage from the same work of Augustine:

> Since God is the highest essence *(summa essencia)*, that is, He is in the highest degree and thus is immutably, He has given being to the things He has created from nothing, but not Being in the highest degree such as He is . . . He has set in order by degrees the natures of essences, for, as from "to be wise" *(sapere)* "wisdom" *(sapiencia)* gets its name, so from "to be" *(esse)* "essence" *(essencia)* gets its name, a new name, however, which the ancient authors of Latin speech did not use, but employed in our day lest there be lacking in our language what the Greeks call *ousian*. For this word is derived from the verb, so that "essence" might be expressed . . .[32]

It is hardly possible to exaggerate the influence of this Augustinian vocabulary of being on that of Boethius, particularly in the presence of the perspectives of Aquinas. In the present context our translation of *esse* must reflect both the Augustinian-Boethian usage and that of Thomas Aquinas. This identification of "being" with "essence" (and indeed with "substance") is to be found in Augustine's *On the Trinity* 5.2.3. and 7.4.9, to mention only a few such places.

A related position, common to Augustine and Boethius in their philosophical analysis of being, is the adjustment of Plato's "theory of the Forms" to a biblical context. Augustine held that those multiple and

---

31. ". . . tanquam in eius comparatione, qui uere est quia incommutabilis est, ea quae mutabilia facta sunt non sint, uehementer hoc Plato tenuit et diligentissime commendauit. Et nescio utrum hoc uspiam reperiatur in libris eorum, qui ante Platonem fuerunt, nisi ubi dictum est: *Ego sum* . . . ," *De ciuitate dei* 8.11; CCSL 47, edd. B. Dombart, A. Kalb <ad fidem qvartae editionis Tevbnerianae . . . paucis emendatis> (Turnhout: 1955), p. 228, ll. 47–52.

32. "Cum enim Deus summa essentia sit, hoc est summe sit, et ideo inmutabilis sit: rebus, quas ex nihilo creauit, esse dedit, sed non summe esse, sicut est ipse; et aliis dedit esse amplius, aliis minus, atque ita naturas essentiarum gradibus ordinauit (sicut enim ab eo, quod est sapere, uocatur sapientia, sic ab eo, quod est esse, uocatur essentia, nouo quidem nomine, quo usi ueteres non sunt Latini sermonis auctores, sed iam nostris temporibus usitato, ne deesset etiam linguae nostrae, quod Graeci appellant *ousian;* hoc enim uerbum e uerbo expressum est, ut diceretur essentia); . . ." *De ciuitate dei* 12.2; CCSL 48, pp. 357, ll. 7–16.

eternal patterns of created realities could be subsumed within a biblical
acceptance of divine unity by understanding them as eternal divine
ideas.[33]

Augustine on Evil as Non-Being. The second Augustinian theme concerning which the indebtedness of Boethius is particularly visible in the
present "dogmatic chapter" pertains to the anti-Manichean effort of
Augustine to refute the dualist doctrine that "good" substances are
matched by "evil" substances. For the Manichees had taught him, and
for nine years he had accepted, the notion that there are two divinities,
one good and one evil; the struggle between that benign god and the
evil anti-god had produced two sorts of substances, some good, produced by the benign divinity, some evil, products of a demonic oppo-
nent. As a convert to Christianity, Augustine was committed to the
Genesis account of creation by the one Lord, himself Good without lim-
it, who, step by step, saw his creation to be good and even "very good"
(Gn 1:1–31). Hence the Bishop of Hippo could write in his *Confessions*
7.14.20: "There is no sanity in those whom any one of Your creatures
displeases . . ."; still, for almost a decade, "my soul . . . had gone over to
the opinion of two substances, but there found no rest . . ."[34] When
Thomas Aquinas would propose an answer to the claim that the presence of evil in our world is incompatible with the reality of the infinite
Good that the God of faith is claimed to be (*Summa theologiae,*1.2.3, response to the first argument) he was content to cite Augustine,
Enchiridion, ch. 11, to the effect that God, both as the Highest Good and
as omnipotent, can bring good out of evil; else He could not tolerate any
evil in the world. Augustine's explicit and often-repeated claim that
"evil" is not a substance, but merely a privation, has consequences in
the order of being and in the order of morality: "A nature which is corrupted is said to be 'evil,' for what is not corrupt is good indeed . . . But

33. See Augustine, *De diversis quaestionibus LXXXIII liber unus,* quaestio 46;
CCSL 44A, ed. A. Mutzenbecher (Turnhout: 1975), p. 70, l. 1-p. 73, l. 73.
34. "Non est sanitas eis, quibus displicet aliquid creaturae tuae, sicut mihi
non erat, cum displicerent multa, quae fecisti. Et quia non audebat anima mea,
ut ei displiceret deus meus, nolebat esse tuum quidquid ei displicebat. Et inde
ierat in opinionem duarum substantiarum et non requiescebat et aliena loque-
batur." *Confessionum,* ed. cit., p. 106, ll. 1–5.

the very nature that is corrupt, insofar as it is a nature, is good; insofar as it is corrupt, it is evil";[35] ". . . no nature at all is evil; the term names nothing but a 'privation of good.'"[36]

This negative ontology of evil grounds a moral perspective in which a sin is fundamentally a "love of nothing." Thus Augustine characterized his paradigmatic sin of stealing pears, not because he and his friends were hungry, but merely to do what was wrong: They had "loved the theft itself" and they had loved their "fellowship" in sin; the pears were "nothing"—thrown away uneaten—and the fellowship in sin was "nothing" either.[37] The theme of substances which are "good," along with the theme of "being," infinitely superior in the divine Essence, infinitely reduced in creatures, constitute a Boethian effort to reap a harvest from Augustinian seeds.

"On the Hebdomads"

With this background in place it is now possible to state in summary form the thrust of the "dogmatic chapter" which was known throughout the Middle Ages under the title Thomas Aquinas accepted, *On the Hebdomads*. In our day this work is generally called by the long and somewhat unwieldy title *How Are Substances Good In This, That They Are, Since They Are Not Substantial Goods?* Both versions of the title derive from the opening lines of the treatise itself (see below, L.1.B1–5; see p. lxvii below for explanation of our abbreviations) and so it is hardly necessary to adjudicate between them; both express literally the intention of Boethius himself. Preference here for the shorter title not only reflects convenience, but is also the occasion for a preliminary clarification without which the work would be unintelligible.

35. "Mala itaque natura dicitur, quae corrupta est: nam incorrupta utique bona est. Sed etiam ipsa corrupta, in quantum natura est, bona est; in quantum corrupta est, mala est." *De natura boni* 4, CSEL 25 (section 6, part 2), ed. J. Zycha (Prague, Vienna, Leipzig: 1892), p. 857, ll. 5–7.

36. ". . . cum omnino natura nulla sit malum nomenque hoc non sit nisi priuationis boni." *De ciuitate dei* 11.22; ed. cit., p. 341, ll. 22, 23.

37. "Non ergo nihil aliud quam furtum amaui; immo uero nihil aliud, quia et illud nihil est." *Confessionum* 2.8.16; ed. cit., vol. 48, p. 25, ll. 6, 7; "At ego illud solus non facerem, non facerem omnino solus. Ecce est coram te, deus meus, uiua recordatio animae meae. Solus non facerem furtum illud, in quo me non libebat id quod furabar, sed quia furabar: quod me solum facere prorsus non liberet, nec facerem." Ibidem, 2.9.17, ed. cit., p. 26, ll. 9–13.

What Is a Hebdomad?

Using the time-honored *topos* of answering a request, our author indicated that he had been asked to solve the difficult question expressed by the longer title and to do so "from our hebdomads *(ex hebdomadibus nostris)*." The first concern of each reader, therefore, has always been to ascertain the meaning of the term "hebdomad," a project on which Alan of Lille was exactly right as to meaning, if somewhat off on etymology: *"ebda"* (there is no such word in Greek) "is said in Greek, *dignitas*, 'worthiness,' in Latin," that is, "worthy of our assent."[38] Alan was right to associate "hebdomad" with "worthiness," that is, the worthiness of a pronouncement to be accepted as self-evidently true, since such is precisely the Greek source, *axios, -a, -on,* "worthy," of our loan-word "axiom" via the Greek *axioma*. Innocent of Greek though they were, all the mediaeval commentators on this work of Boethius were reasonably correct on the meaning of his term "hebdomad." All held that what Boethius had meant by his phrase "from our hebdomads" was "from axiomatic statements," statements he could describe as such that no one who understood them could rationally deny. The formula of Boethius himself is a straight translation of the Stoic *koinai ennoiai*, "common conceptions."[39] A gratuitous difficulty for his mediaeval readers was that they were faced with the mysterious term "hebdomad," evidently proposed by Boethius as synonymous with "common conception"; they had no notion that "hebdomad" means "a seven," and they were faced by an inac-

---

38. "Hebdam enim Graece, Latine *dignitas*. Unde Boetius librum inscripsit *De hebdomadibus*, quasi de subtilissimis theologorum propositionibus . . . non sunt proponendae rudibus, et introducendis." *Regulae Alani de sacra theologia*, PL 210 622A–B.

39. The Boethian terminology *communis animi conceptio*, "a common conception of the mind," described by him as "a statement which, heard, anyone approves <as true>," *enuntiatio quam quisque probat auditam*, is a straight translation of the Stoic Greek expression *koinai ennoiai*, that is, "mental contents held common." He gave as synonyms *terminos regulasque*, "terms and rules." Clearly he indicated what are also referred to as "axioms"—self-evident assertions and called "axioms" precisely because they are "worthy" of assent, as the Greek derivative "axiom" implies. These, Boethius knew his readers would recognize, are found in the mathematical disciplines as well as in others. Here he is interested in axioms that mark "first philosophy" or "metaphysics."

curate manuscript tradition that listed *nine* axioms/hebdomads—as do modern editions to this day.

Three distinguished twelfth-century philosophizing theologians, all given editions by the late Nikolaus M. Häring, agreed that a "hebdomad" is "a mental conception." Clarembaldus of Arras thought that *ebdo* is the equivalent of the Latin *concipio*, "I conceive"; "some," Clarembaldus assured his readers, thought that in Greek, *eb* means "in" and *domas* means "mind" or "soul."[40] Thierry of Chartres held the same view: "Ebdomas" is a conception of the mind; however, alone of the mediaeval commentators Thierry knew another, and correct, interpretation: Some held it to mean "seven."[41] Gilbert of Poitiers too thought it right to say "'ebdomades,' that is, conceptions."[42]

All were correct in the meaning they gave to the puzzling term; only Thierry had a rumor of the correct etymology. The others indulged the temptation to contrive imaginative "etymologies" of this difficult term. Even more obscure than the term "hebdomad" is the term *esse*, "to be," juxtaposed in the hebdomads with the formula *id quod est* or *quod est*, "that-which-is" or "what is." The clarification Boethius has given in another context ought not to be forgotten. In his second work on Porphyry's introductory essay on the *Categories* of Aristotle, *In Isagoge* 4.14, Boethius asked (and answered) precisely the question one would have wished:

> . . . What is, however, the "to be" *(esse)* of a reality? It is nothing other than the definition, for if anyone be asked of a reality "What is it?" if

---

40. ". . . ebdomadum nomen interpretantes ab *ebdo* Graeco quod latine sonat 'concipio' dicimus derivatum, vel, ut alii autumant, ab *eb* quod dicunt 'in' et *domas* quod est 'anima' compositum." "Expositio super librum Boetii De hebdomadibus" 2.8, in *Life and Works of Clarembald of Arras. A Twelfth-Century Master of the School of Chartres,* ed. Nikolaus M. Häring (Toronto: 1965), p. 194.

41. ". . . EX NOSTRIS EBDOMADIBUS i.e. ex conceptionibus nostris uel cogitationibus. *Ebdomas* proprie dicitur septimana ab *epta* quod est septem." "Fragmentum Admuntense, De hebdomadibus" 2, in *Commentaries on Boethius by Thierry of Chartres and His School,* ed. Nikolaus M. Häring (Toronto: 1971), p. 119. Cf. "Abbreuiatio Monacensis, De hebdomadibus" 9, p. 406.

42. ". . . 'ebdomades,' hoc est conceptiones, nominantur . . ." "Expositio in Boecii librum De bonorum ebdomade," Prologus 10, in *The Commentaries on Boethius by Gilbert of Poitiers,* ed. Nikolaus M. Häring (Toronto: 1966), p. 185.

anyone should wish to point out what that "to be" is *(quod est esse mon-strare voluerit)*, one enunciates the definition.[43]

As will be elaborated on below, no "definition" of the act Aquinas was to designate as *esse*, "to be," or "being," is possible; what can be defined is the "essence," the element Aquinas would see as "potentially" existing definable structure. This basic dissent on the application of the term *esse* faces everyone who deals with the present text, a commentary by Brother Thomas who used the term *esse* in a way totally at odds with the Boethian usage.

Nor is this the end of the confusion. A curious device by mediaeval commentators on Boethius was to juxtapose *quod est*, not with *esse*, as Boethius had done, but with *quo est*, "that by which <a reality> is."

Here it may be noted that when Thomas Aquinas in his turn undertook to set out his own understanding of the Boethian text he was equipped with two resources that only Albert among his predecessors had possessed. The first was the notion of "being" that Avicenna (Ibn Sina, a.d. 980–1037) had proposed. According to this Islamic "Aristotelian," *esse*, the "act of being," in a non-necessary reality is distinct from the "essence," the formal structure of that reality.[44] This non-identity of the definable essence with the mysterious energy by which beings, of themselves merely possible, are actual existents, suggested to Latin readers that there is a non-necessary connection between a created essence and its actual being or existence in the created world; in short, possible beings are contingent, not necessary.

43. ". . . quid est autem esse rei? nihil est aliud nisi definitio. uni cuique enim rei interrogatae 'quid est?' si quis quod est esse monstrare voluerit, definitionem dicit." Boethius, *In Eisagogen Porphyrii in Praedicamenta* (hereafter *In Eisagogen*), ed. secunda, 4.14; CSEL 48, ed. G. Schepss and S. Brandt (Vienna and Leipzig: 1906), p. 273, ll. 12–15. Boethius's view on *esse* will be discussed in detail below.

44. "Nous dirons que pour tout ce qui est être possible, il faut qu'il y ait une quiddité autre que son existence . . ." *Livre de science* 1, p. 174, cited by S. Van Riet in her introductory remarks to an edition of *Liber de philosophia prima sive Scientia divina*, series *Avicenna latinus* (Édition critique, I–IV [Louvain: 1977]) Introduction, vol. 1, p. 78*, note 277; the editor goes on to say on the same page as the note cited: "Thomas d'Aquin est d'accord avec Avicenne sur la distinction réelle de l'essence et de l'existence, mais il se sépare de lui en ce qui concerne la correspondence du logique et du réel . . . [according to Aquinas] tout être fini est réellement composé d'essence et d'être et le rapport qui les unit n'est autre que celui de puissance et d'acte." Loco citato, pp. 78*, 79*.

Even more to the point was the second resource. William of Auvergne, Bishop of Paris from 1228 to 1249 after having taught theology in the University of that city, had insisted in his *On the Trinity* that "being," *esse*, has two meanings; in his vocabulary, it has two *intentiones*. The first meaning is "substance" or "quiddity" or "essence," and the second meaning is "what is expressed through the verb 'is.'"[45] In his Introduction to the translation of the treatise *On Being and Essence* by Aquinas, Professor Armand Maurer has noted that "Although the use of *esse* to mean essence had a long tradition in the Middle Ages, going back at least to Boethius, St. Thomas himself reserved the term *esse* to mean the act of existing."[46] As for the influence of William on Thomas, the same authority wrote: "There can hardly be any doubt that St. Thomas had this book [*De trinitate*] in front of him when he wrote *On Being and Essence*."[47] If Brother Thomas outstripped the Bishop, it must be conceded that Aquinas suffered a verbal limitation; unlike Boethius, Thomas did not know Greek.

This is visible in his well-intentioned effort to come to terms with "hebdomad." As was usual when Saint Thomas attempted to "explain" a Greek term, the Saint's linguistic equipment was not up to the task. As will be seen below, Aquinas was persuaded that where Boethius had written *Ekdomatas vero* what the last Roman had intended was *editiones seu conceptiones* (L.1.A54 "conceptions"; ibidem, 55, 67: "editions"). This groundless interpretation will surprise no one who remembers that in the view of Thomas, a "stone," *lapis, lapidis*, was so called because a stone can "injure" one's "foot," *laedere pedem*. Indeed, the Leonine editors of the *De hebdomadibus*, in discussing the possibility of dating our treatise (Leonine ed., pp. 263b–264b), remind us that in his autograph of the parallel work on the *De trinitate* Aquinas referred to this one as *De epd.*, whereas in his Questions *De veritate* his secretaries wrote "regularly" *ebdomadibus* or, in some places, the abbreviation *ebd*. Incidentally, this variation helped to convince the Editors that the Thomistic treatment of the Boethian *De trinitate* can be assigned with fair certainty to

45. *William of Auvergne. De trinitate*, ed. Bruno Switalski (Toronto: 1976), ch. 1, p. 16, l. 40; ch. 2, pp. 20–21, ll. 48–58.
46. *St. Thomas Aquinas. On Being and Essence*, tr. Armand Maurer, 2d rev. ed. (Toronto: 1968), pp. 15, 16.
47. Ibidem, p. 23.

1257–1259, the first Parisian regency of St. Thomas. This dating, the Editors felt, is further supported by the coincidence in the form of the exposition of the *De trinitate* with the form of his work on Peter Lombard's *Sentences*, the form of "disputed questions." It may be remarked in this regard that the manuscript base for our present treatise includes a number of extremely odd versions of the crucial term, not necessarily faults of Thomas, since scribes were listening to his dictation and with ears accustomed to Latin rather than to Greek: *erdidomi, ekdidomi, epdicomi, ebdidomi.* The Leonine editors have settled reasonably on the best of a bad bargain (see their chart of variants for the terms "ebdomadibus," "ekdomadas," Leonine ed., p. 255). As for a positive hint as to the date of the present exposition, it must be noted that (as the Leonine editors remark, p. 264) the fact that it resembles Albert's work on Denis, the pseudo-Areopagite's *Divine Names*, does not exclude an early date; a text in the hand of Thomas is the source of Albert's work, done during their time together at the Dominican *studium* in Cologne before Brother Thomas became a *sententiarius* at Paris. Once more, the Editors have made the best of an obscure situation in saying that the present work was very probably begun later, but one can hardly be more precise on the date (Leonine ed., p. 264b). As for the limitations of Brother Thomas in the matter of Greek, this was more than outweighed by his metaphysical expertise, an expertise anticipated to a degree by William of Auvergne, Bishop of Paris.

In the structure of the beings we experience, William and Thomas saw contingency in the fact that any instance of a finite essence actually exists, since of itself such an essence is merely possible and therefore indifferent to being and to non-being. This would seem to be the situation expressed by the Latin Avicenna's formula that "being," *esse,* "comes to essence," *accidit essenciae.* Each real being is, therefore, a combination of essence, *essencia,* and of being, *esse,* an instance of potency and act, beyond the combination of form as act with matter as potency which accounts for material essences. This advance beyond Avicenna, with its strong emphasis on the priority of being as act, is already present in the heavily rhetorical, even poetic, analogies of fountains and of clouds glowing with the sun's light, in William of Auvergne's Trinitarian treatise.

In any event, Boethius had dedicated an essay based on his axioms to John, Deacon of the Roman Church. There is every reason to identify this personality with Pope John I, Pope from 523 to 526. As were Boethius and Symmachus, the Pope too was a victim of the Ostrogothic King, Theodoric. John died of hardships endured in exile, an exile imposed upon him for collusion in the alleged plot that had caused the downfall and execution of Boethius and Symmachus.

Although his work was dedicated to a colleague who knew well what a "hebdomad" must be, and although our author lost no time in noting that he did not address himself to the uncultivated masses, Boethius began with some helpful remarks for those who had vague notions of what a "hebdomad," an axiom (or, in another terminology, a "maxim") might be.

Axioms, he noted, are customary in mathematics (one thinks of the Euclidean principles from which the theorems are demonstrated), but they are not restricted to mathematics. In theory accessible to all who are rational, in practice a division must be made between those axioms or maxims that are universally intelligible and those intelligible only to the "learned." Boethius provided an illustration of each sort: "equals subtracted from equals, equals remain"; to see this requires no extensive learning, for its truth imposes itself upon any mind that understands the meaning of the terms involved. That "incorporeals are not in a place" will be grasped only by those erudite enough to handle the conceptions of "incorporeal" and "place."

Here a reader of the received text encounters a first difficulty. At some time in the Middle Ages[48] a scribal slip numbered the paragraph in which Boethius both defined what he meant by an axiom and divided axioms into the universally intelligible and those that only the learned can understand, as if that paragraph were the first axiom of the series. Furthermore, numbers seven and eight in the received text are simple,

---

48. Thus the three commentators named above, Clarembaldus, Thierry, and Gilbert, all have numbered the "hebdomads" in the same way; as stated here immediately, what this listing counts as the "first hebdomad" is not a hebdomad, but the definition of a hebdomad; furthermore, they have numbered as "seven" and "eight" the two members of the periodic sentence which is, in fact, "hebdomad six."

declarative sentences, unlike the compound periodic sentences (or, in one case, two short sentences) in which all the other axiomatic principles are formulated. As a result of these two scribal blunders, the received text presents a list of nine axioms. That the blunder goes back at least to the twelfth century is clear as noted: The commentators cited above worked from just such a text of the Boethian treatise. Should the preliminary paragraph that sets out the definition of an axiom and the division of axioms into the generally intelligible and those intelligible only to the erudite be excluded from the list, as clearly it ought to be, the list is reduced to eight. Should axioms seven and eight of the traditional listing, in harmony with all the rest, be combined to form a single periodic sentence, then a list of seven uniformly complex sentences results.

With this adjustment the obscurity of the term "hebdomad" disappears: It is the Greek word for "seven." Others, of course, have pointed out the grounds for this re-ordering of the axioms. If Porphyry was justified in naming his edition of the essays by Plotinus *Enneads*, that is, "nines," because he had grouped those essays in six blocks of nine essays each, then Boethius and his first readers had every right to name the third tractate *On the Hebdomads*, that is, *On the Sevens*, for he had indeed attempted to solve his problem "from our sevens," *ex hebdomadibus nostris*, from the seven axioms listed.

To avoid confusion, the list of the axioms from which Boethius derived his solution of the problem is here given with two sets of numbers. In accord with the text tradition, Roman numerals are used to number the axioms, but an Arabic numeral identifies them in accord with the two corrections noted above. This entails dropping Roman numeral "I" since, in the received text, that number wrongly identified as the first axiom the paragraph in which Boethius first defined and then divided axioms in general. Roman numerals seven and eight of the received text are combined as Arabic number "six." The translation of the axioms is literal and terms easily mistaken, or the object of controversy, are given in Latin in parentheses as well as in translation. It must be noted also that for the sake of consistency the text translated is that provided by the editors of the Leonine edition of the Thomistic Exposition rather than that found in editions of Boethius.

1 (II)

Being *(esse)* and that which is *(id quod est)* are diverse. For being itself *(ipsum esse)* as yet is not. That-which-is however, once the form of being *(essendi)* has been taken on, is and stands together.

2 (III)

What-is *(quod est)* can participate in something, but being itself *(ipsum esse)* in no way participates in anything. For participation occurs when something already is. Something is, however, when it has received being *(esse)*.

3 (IV)

That-which-is *(id quod est)* can possess something other than what it itself is *(quod ipsum est)*. Being itself, however *(ipsum uero esse)*, has nothing else outside itself as an admixture.

4 (V)

However, to be something *(tamen esse aliquid)*, and to be something in this, that <a thing> is *(esse aliquid in eo quod est)*, are diverse. For by the former *(illic)*, accident is signified; by the latter *(hic)*, substance.

5 (VI)

Everything that is participates in that which is being *(eo quod est esse)* with the result that it be. It participates in something else with the result that it be something. And through this, that-which-is *(id quod est)* participates in that which is being *(eo quod est esse)* with the result that it be. It is, however, with the result that it can participate in anything else you like.

6 (VII–VIII)

In every composite, being *(esse)* is other than the item itself. Every simple item possesses its being *(esse)* and that-which-is *(id quod est)* as one.

7 (IX)

All diversity is discordant, whereas similitude must be sought. And what seeks something else is shown to be itself by nature such as that which it seeks.

Dilemma

Boethius has proceeded to solve his problem by stating first an apparently insoluble dilemma. If real individual beings *(omne quod est)* tend to "the good," then they themselves must be good as well, for "like tends to like," a truth so patent that it has found its place as the last of the axioms, number nine in the received text, seven in the adjusted enumeration. The problem, however, is to show "how" they are good, "in what way," *quomodo.*

Boethius implies that two modes exhaust the possibilities: the Platonic claim, so little acceptable to Aristotle,[49] that the way in which substances are good is "by participation"; alternatively, substances might be good "by substance." Each, he argued, entails a serious speculative objection.

Should substances be good by participation, then this state of affairs is not "of themselves"; this is as much as to say that they are in no way good of or through themselves. The alternative is that substances are good, not by participation, but "by substance," that is, what they are is good and they possess "that which they are" thanks to Boethian being, *esse;* this *esse* thus turns out to be good and consequently, all things are by substance like the First Good. Stated bluntly, this alternative entails the blasphemy that all things are God, a conclusion Boethius found as absurd philosophically as it is sacrilegious.

Good, therefore, neither by participation (for this is not truly to be good) nor by substance (because this would mean that everything is God), substances cannot be good at all: *Nullo modo igitur sunt bona.*

Solution

In a well-known passage of his second commentary on the *Isagoge* of Porphyry, Boethius contrived an "Aristotelian" solution to the problem

---

49. See Aristotle, *Metaphysics* 1.9; 991a19 sqq.

posed by universal predication in a cosmos of individual things.[50] This was to concede that we can think apart what cannot exist apart. Socrates is rightly called "human" even though the universal "human" is not to be found in isolation in the real world. Although "Platonizing," Boethius did not exclude this line of thought from any and all problems. Here in the *De hebdomadibus* Boethius made use of that same distinction. The very property of being a triangle, for instance, can be separated in thought from the underlying matter of any particular triangle.

Since this is so, Boethius here proposed an audacious contrary-to-fact hypothesis. Let us remove in theory the presence of the First Good from our consideration, despite the fact that, as he noted, "all the learned and . . . unlearned, as well as . . . the religions of the barbarous nations" by universal consent acknowledge the divine Reality.

Next, he invites us to stipulate that all real beings are good, but only to the point that this would have been possible on his hypothesis that they have not come forth from the First Good—universally acknowledged, to be sure, but here suppressed for the sake of his philosophical experiment.

It is immediately clear that there is a distinction within every substance that is not the First Good: In such items it is one thing to be and another to be good. The goodness of the item, like its whiteness, heaviness, or rotundity, must be distinct from its substance. If all these traits were the same as the substance of the being they qualify, then weight would be the same as color and good, good the same as weight, which, as Boethius put it, "Nature does not permit to happen."

Thus, for items stipulated not to have come from God, it is not the same thing to be, and to be of a certain sort. Within their very structures, to be what they are and to be good, as well as to be white, heavy, etc., are not the same. On the other hand (reflecting the dichotomy and

50. "sed Plato genera et species ceteraque non modo intelligi uniuersalia, uerum etiam esse atque praeter corpora subsistere putat, Aristoteles uero intelligi quidem incorporalia atque uniuersalia, sed subsistere in sensibilibus putat; quorum diiudicare sententias aptum esse non duxi, altioris enim est philosophiae. idcirco uero studiosius Aristotelis sententiam executi sumus, non quod eam maxime probaremus, sed quod hic liber ad Praedicamenta conscriptus est, quorum Aristoteles est auctor." *In Eisagogen* 1.11, ed. cit., p. 167, ll. 12–20.

dilemma already articulated above), Boethius points out that if things were nothing but good, they could have no weight, no color, no extension, nor any other quality. They would be less "things" than the "Principle of things"; in that case we would not contemplate "them" but "It," for One and One only is Good and nothing but Good. Here, of course, Boethius refers to God.

Since things are not God, they are not simple in their structures. But, the reader here might ask: Is goodness as distinct from substance as are accidents such as whiteness, rotundity, and heaviness, as would be the case, according to Boethius, if things were not from God?

Boethius deals with this in his solution to the dilemma he had posed. Contrary to the impossible hypothesis that things are not from God, finite realities, "secondary goods," could not in fact exist at all except by the Will of the One Who is nothing but Good. Because they flow from the Will of the Good Itself, their being is good. In short, the First Good is Good insofar as He is, just because of What He is, which is Goodness Itself; the secondary good is good also, and good just insofar as it is, but only because its being flows from Him Whose Being is the Good.

There is no doubt that for an item to be good insofar as it is, is for it to be good in a very profound way. Still, according to Boethius, finite things are not similar to the First Good, for their being is not good in "whatever way things may be"; they are not "nothing else at all except Good," that is, they are not Goodness Itself. In their very dependence upon the First Good they differ from Him and so are less than He. But since they are from the First Good, they do not simply participate in goodness as they might if they were not from God. Rather, they "possess" their "very being . . . as good."

Again, since finite things actually exist because they are produced by the First Good, it follows both that they are good in this, that they are (or good insofar as they are)—which is to say that their being is good—but also that they are not "like" the First Good. For in Him Being and Goodness are absolutely identical, and He is identical with all that He is. He is Being Itself and Goodness Itself.

This point leads us to pause here for some interpretation before finishing our summary. A question remains that Boethius does not seem to have addressed squarely. Are finite beings, creatures, good by substance

or by participation? Clearly they are not merely "good by participation" in one sense of that term, for this is the only way they might be good, according to Boethius, if they were *not* from the First Good. Now Boethius contrasts being good by participation with being good insofar as a thing is, and, as has been made evident, for him creatures are good insofar as they are, owing to the fact that they are from God.

Note, however, that when Boethius uses the term "participation" in the text following the axioms, i.e. , in the statement of the dilemma and its solution, he uses this term in the sense of "accidental participation." In this way, for a creature to participate is for it to have traits such as whiteness or rotundity or heaviness, all of which are accidents. In axioms 4 (V) and 5 (VI) Boethius speaks of this type of participation. However, in axiom 5 (VI) he also speaks of a concrete thing's participating in *esse* so that it might *be* (rather than just be *something*, such as white or heavy). We shall return below to this other notion of participation; the point here is that Boethius denies that finite beings are good only in the way in which they are white or round. They are good in a more profound way.

But are they good by substance? Boethius seems to deny this, because then they would seem to be God, "which it is wicked to say." But it must be kept in mind that Boethius is setting up a dilemma which seems to entail that things are not good at all! As has been seen, he does not hold this; nor does he hold that things are good neither by participation nor by substance. To be sure, they are not good merely by participation in the sense of accidental participation, and they are not good by substance as the Good is—they are not Goodness Itself. The question is: Can they be good by participation, or by substance, or in both ways, but in other senses of "good by participation" and "good by substance"?

In axiom 4 (V) Boethius associates "substance" with "to be something in this, that <a thing> is." It would seem to follow that to be substantially *good* is to be *good* in this, that a thing is (or to be good insofar as a thing is); that this is the view of Boethius becomes evident as the treatise continues. When Boethius proposes the dilemma he says that if things are good by participation then of themselves they are not good and hence do not tend to the good. This refers to axiom 7 (IX) in which he had said that things are by nature *(naturaliter)* like that which they

seek, so Boethius is identifying "good by itself" with "good by nature." Boethius then says that things *do* tend to the good (this is the common opinion of the learned); it follows that of themselves, or by nature, things must be good; hence they are good by substance and not by participation. Up to this point it seems that "good by substance," "good by itself" and "good by nature" are identified. But then Boethius goes on to associate being substantially good with being nothing but good, with being Goodness Itself, something he must deny of creatures. As has been seen, for Boethius there is no question that finite beings *are* good insofar as they are—i.e., good by substance—and good by nature in that they tend to the good. So "to be good by substance," or "to be substantially good," seems to have two possible meanings: "to be Goodness Itself," which can be said only of God, and "to be good insofar as a thing is," which is affirmed also of creatures.

But how can this be? How can a creature be substantially good and not be Goodness Itself? Boethius's answer seems to be that in creation the very principle within a creature according to which it is, its *esse,* nature, or form, takes on goodness, so that the creature is good by that which makes it to be what it is, and thus to be. Still, the creature is not Goodness Itself. But then, are creatures not also in some way good by participation? Recall, in axiom 5 (VI) Boethius speaks of a creature's participation in *esse* so that it is—a more profound type of participation than accidental participation. Now we know from the other axioms that every finite and composite being, every *id quod est* that is not God, participates in its principle of being; it is not identical with it. If then, this principle somehow becomes good in the process of creation, the creature may be said to be good, not only substantially in the sense proposed above, but also by participation insofar as it participates in its form which is not identical with, but rather has or possesses, goodness.

In the last part of the *De hebdomadibus* Boethius makes the following final points. One might suppose that because God wills things to be, for example, white, they must be white insofar as they are. Boethius meets this objection by pointing out that God is Good, but not white. Thus creatures are good insofar as they are because God, their source, is Good, or better, because God is Goodness; they are not white insofar as they are, since God is not white.

Yet God is the Just, too: Are all things just insofar as they are? No, be-

cause everything but God is composite; in God to be and to act are identical; not so in creatures. To be just pertains to action whereas, even in
creatures, to be good "pertains to essence" *(essenciam . . . respicit)*. Creatures, therefore, are not just insofar as they are; rational finite beings
may choose to act justly, but they are simply created as good. It should
be clear by now that in speaking of goodness Boethius is not referring to
moral goodness; this would pertain to acting as justice pertains to a special class of actions, a moral "species."

This last section appeals to our understanding of the distinction between God, the Simple Being referred to in the axioms, and creatures,
all of which are composite. It is striking that here for the first time in this
treatise Boethius uses the term *essencia* and does so in the context of his
claim that goodness pertains to it. *Essencia,* of course, is but another term
for form or nature.

Crucial Notions in Boethius

The Boethian Meaning of "Esse"

With this survey in place it is now possible to review with relative
ease a controversy which has arisen with respect to what Boethius intended by his term *esse,* literally "to be." Did Boethius mean by *esse* "the
act of being," the intention attributed to him by Thomas Aquinas, or did
he mean by that term "the essence" which exists? Serious contemporary
authors are to be found to favor each side, and to propose either interpretation is to engage in the harsh duty noted by Aristotle in his
Nicomachean Ethics 1.6; 1096a16–18: As between our friends and truth,
both dear to us, "piety requires us to honor truth above our friends."[51]

---

51. For a survey of major views on the interpretation of *esse* and *id quod est* up
to 1945 see James Collins, "Progress and Problems in the Reassessment of
Boethius," *The Modern Schoolman* 23.1 (November 1945), pp. 16–19. Ralph
McInerny, in his book *Boethius and Aquinas* (Washington, D.C.: 1990), discusses
other authors as well; see esp. pp. 161–98. McInerny disagrees with what we call
the "traditional interpretation," i.e., the view that by *esse* Boethius meant
"essence" or "form."

The reader might also find of interest L.M. De Rijk's article "On Boethius's
Notion of Being," in *Meaning and Inference in Mediaeval Philosophy: Studies in
Memory of Jan Pinborg,* ed. Norman Kretzmann, Synthese Historical Library, vol.
32 (Dordrecht/Boston/London: 1988), pp. 1–29.

As we have seen above, Augustine, who identified "being" with "essence," was the acknowledged Master of Boethius. More than once Augustine asserted that the ultimate excellence of divine Being consists in this that the Holy One is immutable;[52] undergoing no change, divinity does not cease to be what divinity had been, does not begin to be what divinity had not been. "Because God is Good, whatever in some degree is, is from Him—Who is not in some degree, but is IS."[53] Unlike any and all creatures, the Holy One alone merits the Name "Being"; in comparison with the Creator, created beings are as if they were not.[54] The above explication of Boethius's treatise reveals our interpretation of his notion of *esse:* It was said that in the process of creation that principle within a creature according to which it is—its *esse,* nature, or form—becomes good. What further reasons can be adduced for holding that according to Boethius *esse* is form rather than the act of being?

The import of such a question may not be obvious to one unfamiliar with St. Thomas's basic metaphysical principles. For him, as for Aristotle, essence or form is a principle of being; in substances composed of matter and form the latter is the actualizing, the structuring principle. Because nothing can be without being something, to be a this or a that—a tree, or a squirrel—is to be. But, as has been noted, Aquinas pushed further: Essence, whatness itself, is in potency to a further actualizing principle, the act of being, *esse:*

> Being itself *(ipsum esse)* is the most perfect of all, for it is compared to all things as their act *(actus);* for nothing has actuality except insofar as it is. Hence being itself is the actuality *(actualitas)* of all things, even of their forms.[55]

52. *De trinitate* 5.2.3, ed. W.J. Mountain, CCSL 50, 50A (Turnhout: 1968); *De ciuitate dei* 12.2, ed. cit., vol. 48, pp. 356–57.

53. ". . . spiritum sanctum, qui datus est nobis, per quem uidemus, quia bonum est, quidquid aliquo modo est: ab illo enim est, qui non aliquo modo est, sed est est." *Confessionum* 13.31.46, ed. cit., p. 269, l. 24–p. 270, l. 2.

54. "Et inspexi cetera infra te et uidi nec omnino esse nec omnino non esse: esse quidem, quoniam abs te sunt, non esse autem, quoniam id quod es non sunt." Ibidem, 7.11.17, ed. cit., p. 104, ll. 1–3.

55. ". . . ipsum esse est perfectissimum omnium: comparatur enim ad omnia ut actus. Nihil enim habet actualitatem, nisi inquantum est: unde ipsum esse est actualitas omnium rerum, et etiam ipsarum formarum." *Summa theologiae* (hereafter *ST*) 1.4.1 ad 3; see also 1.44.1; 1.50.2 ad 3.

As will be seen, for Aquinas being *(esse)* and goodness are the same in reality, differing only in concept. Aquinas's doctrine of being thus enables him to locate the goodness of the creature in its very act of being and, as we shall explain, provides a most satisfactory solution to the problem posed by Boethius in the *De hebdomadibus*. If Boethius had entertained this same notion of *esse*, including this understanding of its relation to goodness, his answer would almost certainly be identical with that of Aquinas. Now, as will be seen, Aquinas does claim that by *esse* Boethius also means "act of being"; the Angelic Doctor offers his own solution to the dilemma posed in the *De hebdomadibus* as emerging from the way he claims Boethius uses *esse*. If, then, Boethius meant by *esse* what Aquinas meant, the Angelic Doctor's explication of Boethius's treatise would be simply an elaboration on what, in fact, Boethius intended to say. If, on the other hand, Boethius meant by *esse* "essence," Aquinas's commentary is a *creative* elaboration which anticipates his own fully developed teaching on being and goodness.

One must reject the temptation to suppose that Boethius means whatever Aquinas says he means. Rather, Boethius's views must be examined independently, and only then can questions concerning Aquinas's attribution of his meaning of *esse* to Boethius be considered. These questions include the following. If Boethius means by *esse* what Aquinas means, why have so many scholars denied it? As will be seen, this interpretation poses numerous textual problems. On the other hand, if Boethius means by *esse* form or nature, why would Aquinas attribute to his predecessor a stance not really taken by him? Indeed, one might even wonder if Aquinas knew what Boethius himself thought.

To be sure, Aquinas as an interpreter and scholar cannot be ignored. But neither must one assume that he would not bestow upon *his* teachers more credit than what *we* perhaps think is due. We shall return to this point, but let us now examine further Boethius's notion of *esse* in the *De hebdomadibus*.

Since many scholars have proffered the interpretation of Boethius with which we agree, we shall call it the "traditional interpretation." Evidence is adduced based on historical influences as well as textual analysis. The former type of evidence is crucial, as our previous comments suggest; an understanding of the thought of those to whom a lat-

er author referred, whom he studied and revered, provides indispensable starting points for approaching the texts of the author in question. But the basis for determining whether and to what extent someone or something *is* an influence on that author must include a close analysis of those texts. This includes comparing various works to search for common teachings, as well as attempting to find consistency of thought within a particular work.

In an author such as Boethius this is not an easy task. Keep in mind that he was attempting to reconcile Plato and Aristotle; this fact alone may account for why scholars disagree on what Boethius believed about the ontological status of universals.[56] Moreover, in different works Boethius uses the same term in different ways; indeed, he does this even within the same work. Although context often clarifies what might otherwise be confusing, room for interpretation sometimes remains. Below we shall illustrate with a few examples how Boethius uses terms in different ways and how context helps resolve questions concerning his meaning. We shall then attempt to justify our interpretation of Boethius's use of *esse* by comparisons with other works and by appealing to Boethius's general consistency of teaching on certain issues. Some arguments of previous scholars will be re-presented. Finally, we

56. Henry Chadwick, who traces Neoplatonic influences on Boethius, says "both in his second commentary on Porphyry and in the fifth tractate" Boethius has occupied the Aristotelian position that "universals have being solely as instantiated in the particulars that compose them" (Chadwick, p. 215). We have above addressed this point regarding the second commentary on the Isagoge of Porphyry. Here a few passages regarding Boethius's Platonic stance may prove enlightening. In his *On the Topics of Cicero (In Ciceronis Topica)*, Boethius says, "As the best philosophers agree, the things that really exist are those which are thoroughly isolated from the senses, and those which supply beliefs for the senses exist less truly: . . . ut inter optime philosophantes constitit, illa maxime sunt quae longe a sensibus segregata sunt, illa minus, quae opiniones sensibus subministrant." *Boethius's* In Ciceronis Topica, tr. Eleonore Stump (Ithaca and London: 1988, hereafter *ICT*), p. 86; PL 64 1092). In his *Consolation of Philosophy* 3, pr. 12 Boethius declares that he strongly agrees with Plato; in 5, pr. 4 he speaks of the reason's ability to grasp the simple form itself. In his *De trinitate* Boethius says that forms in matter are better termed "images"; he states "from these forms which are outside matter have come those forms which are in matter and produce a body: Ex his . . . formis quae praeter materiam sunt, istae formae venerunt quae sunt in materia et corpus efficiunt." *De trin.* 2, ll. 48–56 in *The Theological Tractates*.

shall contrast with Aquinas's solution the overall solution Boethius gives to the dilemma that he poses. Comments on Aquinas's attributing to Boethius a meaning not held by him will close our discussion of *esse* in Boethius.

One of the most striking examples of Boethius's use of a term to signify different things concerns the term *id quod est*. It has been seen that in the *De hebdomadibus* this term signifies a concrete being or, in Aristotelian terminology, a "primary substance."[57] In the *De trinitate* Boethius says that since God is pure form, not form and matter, He is what He is, *id quod est*. But other things are not what they are, *id quod sunt*.[58] The context makes it clear that *id quod est* here ascribed to creatures refers to whatness or essence—the Aristotelian "*secondary* substance"—since *if* it referred to the concrete being itself, as it does in the *De hebdomadibus*, every *id quod est* indeed *would* be *id quod est*, its very self. Despite the distinct meanings of this important term, Boethius does not explain, or even allude to, his variant usage.

Even in the same work Boethius shifts meanings, or employs words with more than one meaning, without warning. The term "substance" is often so used—here, for primary substance, there, for secondary substance. For example, Christ is one substance, yet has two substances, or natures.[59] Moreover, predicating, for example, justice of God (God is the Just, or Justice) is in the *De trinitate* at times said to be substantial predication, at other times, beyond-substantial.[60] In the short treatise on substantial predication in the Trinity, *Whether Father, Son, and Holy Spirit Are Substantially Predicated of the Trinity*, by "substantial predication" Boethius refers to the predication of a term that is applicable to each and to all Persons of the Trinity—such as "God," "Truth," "Justice," but not

---

57. Since until axiom 6, VII–VIII, *id quod est* is described as a subject of accidents, it cannot in the first five axioms be essence or form, for Boethius holds that forms cannot be substrates: *De trin.* 2, ll. 42–51. In axiom 6, VII–VIII, *id quod est* continues to stand for a being, but here the term becomes broader, standing as well for a simple being. Of course God is the simple being, Who cannot be a substrate: *Contra Eutychen et Nestorium* (hereafter *CE*) in *The Theological Tractates*, 3, ll. 95–101.

58. *De trin.* 2, ll. 29–42; 4, ll. 24–36.

59. *CE* 7, ll. 91–103; also 4, ll. 54–59.

60. *Ultra substantiam: De trin.* 4, ll. 9–44; 105–8. This translates the Greek *hyperousian*.

"Trinity."[61] In this dogmatic treatise Boethius did define "substantial predication," but even in the absence of that definition his examples would make his meaning evident.

Sometimes a little more reflection is required to ascertain the meaning of a term; still, fairly certain conclusions can be drawn. For example, we have seen that *id quod est* is used in the *De trinitate* for whatness, or essence. However, Boethius seems also to have a less technical sense for the equivalent term *quod est*. When he contrasts God and humans, pointing out that God is pure form, purely His essence, purely God, he says that, on the other hand, man is not simply or purely man, for what he is, *quod est*, he owes to other things which are not man, that is, which are not humanity (*De trin.* 4, ll. 24–36). *Quod est* here apparently signifies all that constitutes the concrete being, in this case, the individual human being. For any material (and therefore composite) being this would include matter and accidents, as well as form. There is an interesting parallel in Boethius's use of *esse* in the same work. He holds that God is pure *esse* and form (*De trin.* 2, ll. 18–21). But he also says that each composite being that is not what it is (i.e., that is not purely its essence) has its *esse* from its parts.[62] Whatever *esse* means here—it seems to signify something like "actual being or existence"—it clearly does not refer to God. Neither does it mean "form," nor does it indicate a distinct principle of being, each of which in some sense would be a part, at least as opposed to the conjunction of all the principles that structure the concrete reality. One might point out that the non-technical "what," *quod,* seems to focus on the components, while the non-technical *esse* suggests the existing aspect of the components. This appears to be puzzling, but truly what our author means.

Surely Boethius was aware of the notion of actual existence. We see it expressed in the *De hebdomadibus* when he stresses that creatures could not actually exist *(actu . . . exsistere)* unless willed by the First Good. In the *De trinitate* Boethius holds that God is form and *esse* and the source of *esse;* "all *esse* is from form, *omne . . . esse ex forma est"* (*De trin.* 2, ll. 17–21). True, we shall argue that the *esse* of which God is the source

---

61. In *The Theological Tractates,* ll. 27–57.
62. ". . . habet esse suum ex his ex quibus, id est ex partibus suis . . .": see *De trin.* 2, ll. 31–37.

and which comes from form is the embodied essence of creatures. But even if in the context of the quotation *esse* means nothing but the actual being of things, their actually being out there, in the world, that does not entail the conclusion that Boethius proposes *esse* as a distinct metaphysical principle. Nor can one legitimately conclude without further evidence that for Boethius every composite existent has the two principles of essence and *esse* corresponding to the non-technical meanings of *quod est* and *esse* discussed above.

Let us now attempt to justify our interpretation of *esse* as essence, or form, as that term *(esse)* is used in the *De hebdomadibus*. Other scholars have drawn parallels between passages from the *De trinitate* and the *De hebdomadibus*, and these merit repeating here. As already noted, in the *De trinitate* Boethius claims that God is what He is, is form, is His essence, although a man is not (purely) what he is; he is not humanity.[63] In the *De hebdomadibus* Boethius says that, in the case of composite things, the thing or item is not its *esse;* rather *id quod est,* the concrete being, and *esse* are diverse (axioms 1, II; 6, VII–VIII). In the Simple Being however, *id quod est* and *esse* are one.[64] Of course, as becomes clear from Boethius's solution in his *De hebdomadibus,* the Simple Being is God, while His creatures are composite. Thus, while in the *De trinitate* God is said to be identical with His form or essence, in the *De hebdomadibus* He is said to be identical with His *esse.* And while in the *De trinitate* creatures are said to be more than their essence, in the *De hebdomadibus* they are said to participate in something beyond *esse* (axiom 5, VI).

Moreover, accidents are what creatures participate in beyond *esse:* This is clear from axioms 4 (V) and 5 (VI) of the *De hebdomadibus.* Now in the *De trinitate* Boethius speaks of humans as having parts, as having components which are not man, *aliis quae non sunt homo.*[65] The parts mentioned are soul and body, but he also, throughout the tractate, contrasts God with beings having accidents; the latter beings must be material, since forms cannot be substrates (*De trin.* 2, ll. 42–51). Such material, composite beings result from the composition of form and matter

63. *De trin.* 2, ll. 29–42; 4, ll. 24–36.
64. One commentator who has argued along these lines is Pierre Duhem, in *Le système du monde,* vol. 5 (Paris: 1917), pp. 288–89.
65. *De trin.* 2, ll. 32–37; 4, ll. 33–34.

—or, more precisely, from God's joining form and matter (*De trin.* 2, ll. 51–53). Recall that the first axiom (1, II) in the *De hebdomadibus* says that once *esse* is taken on, a (composite) being is.

Again, Boethius's claim in the *De trinitate* that forms cannot be substrates is parallel to axiom 2 (III), which says that what is *(quod est)* can participate in something, but being itself *(ipsum esse)* in no way participates,[66] and axiom 3 (IV) in which Boethius holds that *esse* has *(habet)* nothing outside itself as an admixture.

In the *De trinitate* Boethius denotes the "forms" that are in bodies as not, strictly speaking, forms, but rather as "images" *(imagines)* of the genuine forms. From these forms which are outside matter, he says, have come those forms which are in matter and produce a body (*De trin.* 2, ll. 48–56). This sounds as though Boethius holds that forms proper have a separate existence; yet in the *De hebdomadibus* he says that *esse* (alone) is not—that is, does not exist—but the concrete (composite) be-ing is, once it has received *esse* (axiom 1, II). We know that Boethius was well aware of the difference between Plato and Aristotle on the separate existence of forms; despite his apparent ambiguity on the subject, the *De trinitate* shows that he sides with Plato.[67] As a Christian he had only to follow Augustine: Boethius would locate the forms within the mind of God, as exemplars.[68] Now since, in the *De hebdomadibus, esse* is denied a be-ing separate from the *id quod est,* if *esse* is somehow form, it could not

66. If "participation" in this axiom is taken in Boethius's general sense of that term, it includes the notion of "accidental participation," which is discussed further in the subsequent axioms.

67. Boethius explains the difference between Plato and Aristotle on forms in, e.g., *ICT*, p. 103 (PL 64 1106). In addition to places already cited supporting Boethius's Platonism, see *CE* 3, ll. 29–62, where he discusses the difference between "to subsist" *(subsistere)*, which he associates with "to be" *(esse)*, and "to substand" *(substare)*. Something has subsistence when it does not require accidents in order to be; genera and species thus subsist. A substance functions as a substrate to accidents. Individuals *(individua)* subsist and substand. God subsists, and one may say He substands not because He is a substrate, but because He is the Principle beneath all things, giving them subsistence (ibidem, ll. 87–101).

In these passages, along with ll. 63–86, Boethius also associates essence *(essencia)* and being *(esse)*. He points out that we can say appropriately that man has essence, because he is; God is essence, for He is and is especially that from which proceeds the being of all things.

68. Aquinas himself points this out: *ST* 1.65.4 ad 1.

be the pure form spoken of in *De trinitate* 2, for such pure form does have being elsewhere, i.e., in God. But Boethius's distinction between forms outside bodies and forms in matter provides the solution: *Esse* is embodied form, the principle of the being of the composite entity.

In the section of the *De trinitate* treated above in which Boethius discusses God as pure form, our author points out that attributes predicated of God are the same as His substance, which is really beyond substance *(ultra substantiam)*. Humans may be just, but God is Justice; creatures may be great, He is Greatness Itself. With regard to his teaching on predication, Boethius was again following Augustine. For example, Augustine, in his *De trinitate* (especially book 5, chapters 10–11), asserts that in God to be is to be great; God is Greatness. In book 7 he also says that, because in the simplicity of God to be wise is not different from to be, there wisdom is the same as essence (7.1.2). This is because essence is that by which something is.

Now when Augustine says that because to be wise is (the same as) to be, wisdom is the same as essence, he was speaking only of God, for God alone is His essence, which is the same as Wisdom, Greatness, and Goodness. But, as already noted, Augustine also stresses another claim, familiar to neoplatonists and central to Christianity: Everything, insofar as it is, is good. Might one such as Boethius not question whether this claim is equivalent to "to be is (the same as) to be good"? If so—that is, patterned on the assertion that if to be is the same as to be wise, then essence equals wisdom—it would seem that even the essence of a creature would be goodness. For if to be is the same as to be good, then essence equals goodness. But this is impossible for creatures. If such an apparent paradox occurred to Boethius, it is not surprising that in his *De trinitate* justice and greatness are discussed as substantial predicates, whereas goodness is mentioned only once, at the end of the treatise. Nor is it surprising that another tractate, the *De hebdomadibus,* should have been written to explore the problem that seems to arise from the aforementioned teachings of Augustine: How can substances be good insofar as they are, since they are not substantial goods, i.e., Goodness Itself?

A few more brief points supporting the traditional interpretation of *esse* according to Boethius will be offered here: All become clearer by

comparison with Aquinas's teaching, either in general, or as it is presented in his *Exposition* of the *De hebdomadibus*.

In the *De hebdomadibus* Boethius says

> Of those things . . . whose substance is good, that which they are *(id quod
> sunt)* is good. That which they are, however, they possess from that
> which is being *(ex eo quod est esse)*. Therefore their being *(esse)* is good;
> therefore, the very being of all things is good. But if \<their> being is
> good, those things that are, are good insofar as they are, and for them to
> be is the same as to be good *(idemque illis est esse quod boni esse).*[69]

The language in this quotation leaves no room for doubt: The formula *id
quod sunt* means "that which they are," i.e., *what* they are; thus Boethius
is claiming that what things are comes from their *esse*. If *esse* referred to
an act of being, Boethius would be explaining that the whatness of a
thing proceeds from its act of being. But this unusual assertion is opposed to Boethius's teaching in the *De trinitate* 2, 1. 21: All being *(esse)* is
from form. Whatever *esse* may mean here, form as its source is clearly
indicated.

It is instructive to examine Aquinas's gloss of this passage. As noted
in passing above, and as will be discussed further below, Aquinas attributes to Boethius a notion of *esse* as "act of being." How, then, does
Aquinas deal with Boethius's claim that whatness comes from *esse?* He
omits one crucial word, *id,* so that *his* version of the passage reads "But
that certain things might 'be,' this *they possess from that which is being (sed
quod aliqua sint, hoc habent ex eo quod est esse)."*[70] Aquinas continues, "for it
was said above that something is when it has received 'to be' *(esse)."*[71]

In his tractate on the Person and natures of Christ *(Against Eutyches
and Nestorius, Contra Eutychen et Nestorium)* Boethius refutes both the er-

---

69. "Quorum vero substancia bona est id quod sunt bona sunt. Id quod sunt
autem habent ex eo quod est esse. Esse igitur ipsorum bonum est. Omnium igitur rerum ipsum esse bonum est. Set si esse bonum est ea que sunt in eo quod
sunt bona sunt. Idemque illis est esse quod bonis esse." L.3.B14–19. The Leonine
text of Boethius here is slightly different from Stewart, Rand, and Tester, but not
significantly so.

70. L.3.A108–109; McInerny translates this passage differently: *Boethius and
Aquinas,* pp. 175, 222.

71. ". . . dictum est enim supra quod est aliquid cum esse susceperit."
L.3.A109–110.

ror of Nestorius, who held that there are two natures and two persons in Christ, and that of Eutyches, who believed that in Christ there is one Person and only one nature, the Divine. Although presenting the orthodox view of one eternal divine Person and two natures, the divine and the human, Boethius proffers no notion of an act of being *(esse)* of Christ, the Second Person, as Aquinas would later do.[72] True, Boethius does affirm that one *(unum)* and *esse* are convertible, for whatever is one, is; but this is done in the context of showing that if Christ is two persons, He is nothing at all, for to be, something must be one.[73] Yet if our author has a distinct notion of the act of being, it would be appropriate and even expected for this to be alluded to in so technical a treatise on the reality of the Incarnate Word.

It has already been noted that the Simple Being for Boethius is God; this is made clear from the following passage from the *De hebdomadibus:* "Because they are not simple, they <created things> could not be at all unless That Which alone is Good had willed them to be."[74] That is, non-simple (composite) beings must be willed, as distinct from the Simple Being. Only God is not willed to be, but is from all eternity.[75] Now axiom 6 (VII–VIII) distinguishes two kinds of beings, simple and composite; composite beings can participate in accidents; hence, according to the *De trinitate*, they must include matter in their composition, as has already been noted. But categorizing all composite beings as material, in contrast to the one Simple Being who is God, has its problems. There is no doubt but that Boethius believed in angels,[76] but what metaphysical explanation of them would he offer? If God is the only Simple Being, angels must be composite; but composite beings have matter, and angels do not. As Chadwick has remarked, "Boethius does not show how God as pure form is distinguished from other forms in which there is no ma-

---

72. E.g., *ST* 3.17.1 and 2.

73. *CE* 4, ll. 30–46. Note the apparent priority of oneness; cf. *Con.* 3, pr. 11.

74. "Que quoniam non sunt simplicia nec esse omnino poterant nisi ea id quod solum bonum est esse uoluisset." L.4.B33–34. The passage in Stewart, Rand, and Tester reads the same way.

75. *On the Catholic Faith, De fide catholica* (hereafter *DF*), ll. 55–65, in *The Theological Tractates.*

76. See e.g., *DF,* ll. 66–80; *Con.* 4, pr. 6 (l. 54 in *The Theological Tractates*); *CE* 2, ll. 28, 37.

terial element."[77] But how could he? He could if he, like Aquinas, posited a distinct act of *esse*, so that the composition of an angel would be that of *esse* and essence.[78] However, if Boethius had this notion and if he were using it in the *De hebdomadibus*, would he not have indicated *some* difference in the types of composite beings? Might he not even have indicated how accidental participation could then occur in composite beings that are not material? In expounding axiom 6 (VII–VIII) Aquinas does discuss a sort of being that is simple in that it is not composed of matter and form, yet "not . . . altogether simple *(non . . . omnino simplex).*" In an apparent attempt to maintain as much as possible the neoplatonic flavor of Boethius's work, Aquinas uses examples "following the opinion of Plato *(secundum opinionem Platonis)*": the forms of human beings, and horses, which *if* they subsisted would still participate in *esse*, and thus be composite. Although not directly discussing the manner in which pure forms—for Aquinas, angels—possess accidents, St. Thomas immediately notes that *God* can have no accidents, because He is subsisting *Esse* (L.2.A216–258).

A comparison between Boethius's and Aquinas's solution to the problem posed in the *De hebdomadibus* strikes us as the most convincing evidence that Boethius has no notion of a distinct act of *esse*. To understand this point fully, one must know how Aquinas explains goodness. As there is substantial and accidental being, *esse*, so is there corresponding goodness; for goodness *is* being, and thus differs from being only in concept.[79] To the extent that something is good by substantial being, being in an absolute sense, it is "complete" just insofar as it is: Its essence is

77. Chadwick, p. 215.

78. In Aquinas, see *ST* 1.50.2 ad 3.

79. *ST* 1.5.1, especially ad 1. Places where Aquinas speaks of the being—*esse, ens*—of accidents include *ST* 1.5.3 ad 2; 1.9.2; 1.54.3 ad 3; 3.2.6 ad 2; 3.77.2: *esse;* 1.90.2: *ens*. Aquinas holds that it belongs to accidents to exist only in subjects: in addition to the places just cited, see, e.g., 1.5.5 ad 2; 1.28.2; 1.77.6. For a place where Aquinas uses *bonitas*, "goodness" of creatures (in addition to *bonum*, "good"), see 1.6.3 ad 3.

For a fuller discussion of Aquinas on goodness, see Janice L. Schultz, "Thomistic Metaethics and a Present Controversy," *The Thomist* 52.1 (January 1988), pp. 40–62, and "Is-Ought: Prescribing and a Present Controversy," *The Thomist* 49.1 (January 1985), pp. 1–23. These articles focus on the descriptive notion of "good."

actualized. This being is goodness in a relative sense *(secundum quid)* only; every member of a species is equally good by this account. Although the actuality or being of accidents does not make anything to *be* absolutely but only to be this way or that way, the corresponding notion of goodness is of goodness absolutely *(simpliciter)*, for by accidents a thing can become a complete one of its kind, can actualize its potentiality. This type of actuality or being enables one tree to be better than another, one human to be more developed than another. And so this kind of being or completion is goodness in the proper sense. These points are fully developed in the *Summa theologiae;* in the *Exposition* the two kinds of goodness are discussed directly after Aquinas's treatment of how, according to Boethius, creatures are good thanks to their having proceeded from God.

Below we shall have more to say about the way Aquinas uses *esse* in this *Exposition;* here we shall simply note that he takes *esse* to be the act of being *(actus essendi),* and holds that creatures participate in this act in order to be; he also distinguishes substantial and accidental *esse* (L.2.A54–59, A153–169; L.4.A145–160). Since being and goodness are, for Aquinas, the same in reality, creatures participate in goodness insofar as they participate in being *(esse).*[80] God, on the other hand, is Subsisting Being; He participates in nothing (L.2.A249–258). His *esse* and essence are one; goodness is *esse;* hence, He is Goodness Itself.[81]

Thus Aquinas can simply and elegantly solve Boethius's problem in the following way. God, Who is Being, is Goodness; His Being is His Essence; He is thus essentially good. Creatures have or "participate in" being; hence they are good by being, i.e., insofar as they are. In them, however, being is distinct from essence; thus they are not good by essence, they are not essentially good.[82]

Boethius, who makes no explicit distinction between the *esse* and

80. This point is discussed further below. As noted below, in the *Exposition* Aquinas does not explicitly equate being and goodness, although he suggests this view; nor does he *state* that creatures participate in goodness, even though this is his position, as is clear from *ST:* see below, "Aquinas on Boethius: Goodness."

81. L.4.A150–160; L.5.A42–46. On the simplicity of God in *ST,* see 1.3.6; 1.3.7.

82. L.4.A132–160; *ST* 1.6.3, esp. ad 2 and 3, and 1.6.4. More below on Aquinas's interpretation of Boethius's solution.

essence of a creature, proposes a somewhat tortuous solution. Let us review it. Creatures are not good merely by accidental participation; since,
however, they do participate in their *esse*, and their *esse* becomes good in
the process of creation, they are "good by participation" in another and
deeper sense. Further, creatures are in some way good substantially,
inasmuch as they are good by virtue of their *esse*, although they are not
goodness itself. Boethius does not offer a formulation or description of
the goodness of creatures; below we shall offer a possible interpretation.
Even Aquinas, who, as will be seen, attempts to give Boethius as much
credit as possible for his own solution (most completely expressed in the
Summa theologiae), points out that according to Boethius the *esse* of a
creature is good owing to a relationship to God.[83] *Aquinas* then associates this *esse* with the goodness corresponding to substantial being;[84]
however, when discussing Boethius's own solution, Aquinas does not
actually *equate* this being with goodness.[85]

At this point one might wonder whether Boethius himself some-
where clearly identifies *esse* as essence. One important passage was cited
above. The following are also most revelatory. In his work *On the* Topics
of Cicero (In Ciceronis Topica), Boethius says ". . . the definition shows
what the thing defined is; that is, it shows its substance . . . every definition unfolds what the thing that it defines is. (Aristotle delimited definition in almost exactly the same way: A definition is an expression signi-
fying the being-what-it-is)."[86] In *On Different Topics (De topicis differentiis)*,
Boethius's view of definition is similar: ". . . the definition shows the
substance . . . a definition contains genus and differentiae . . ."[87] Clearly

83. L.4.A135–150; L.5.A11–13.
84. In L.4.A145–160 Aquinas says that a creature is absolutely good insofar
as it is complete in *esse* and operation, but goodness absolutely speaking does *not*
belong to creatures according to their essential "to be," *secundum ipsum esse essenciale eorum.* The implication is that the other type of goodness, goodness in the
relative sense, *does* belong according to this kind of essential or substantial being.
85. Although he says that the being of creatures has the character, *ratio,* of
good because it is from God: L.5.A59–67, 76–79.
86. ". . . sed quid sit, id est ejus quod definit, substantiam monstrat . . . Ergo
omnis definitio explicat quid sit id quod definitur. Aristoteles vero eodem pene
modo definitionem determinat, dicens: Definitio est oratio quid est esse signifi-
cans."; *ICT,* pp. 85–86 (PL 64 1091D–1092A).
87. "Diffinitio . . . substantiam monstrat . . . diffinitio genus ac differentias

"substance" here is used as "essence"; Boethius also associates the question of *quid sit* (what it might be) with definition.[88] Now in the same work Boethius also says, "A definition is discourse which indicates the *esse* of anything," and continues to discuss definition as noted above.[89] So Boethius says that definition indicates essence, and he says that definition indicates *esse*.

But this should not surprise us, given the Augustinian identification of essence and *esse*, and, even with respect to the *De hebdomadibus*, given Boethius's statement that to be good pertains to essence *(essenciam)*. *Esse* and essence are simply interchangeable. True, in the *De hebdomadibus* all but once *esse* is used instead of "essence," but the point of the treatise well may indicate why. Boethius was attempting to explain the profound goodness of actually existent things, creatures good insofar as they *are*. He offered the solution that this goodness is a result of a process of their coming-to-*be* from Goodness Itself. True, *esse* is not itself, for Boethius, the goodness of a creature; it is *Aquinas*, not Boethius, who ultimately insists on the radical coextensivity of goodness and its immediate principle *within* the creature, i.e., its act of being. But *esse* is, for Boethius, the principle that enables the creature both to *be* in the world and somehow to acquire goodness in the process of its creaturely coming-to-be, so that it is *good* just insofar as it *is* a being, albeit created and dependent.

For a thinker such as Aquinas, the notion that being good is a function of coming-to-be from Goodness Itself surely points the way to his own solution. As has been seen, for Aquinas goodness *is* being, *esse*. How large is the step between the view that the creating or making-to-be of something is the conferral of goodness, and that *esse is* goodness? In one sense, not large. Yet Boethius did not maintain that the creature pos-

---

sumit . . . ," PL 64 1187A–1187C; *Boethius's* De topicis differentiis, tr. Eleonore Stump (Ithaca and London: 1978, hereafter *TD*), pp. 49–50.

88. *TD*, p. 84 (PL 64 1209 C); see Stump's note 41 on p. 147. For Aristotle on definition, see *Topics* 101b38; 139a28–29; Stump, p. 238. See also p. 104, note 48: *to ti ein einai* in Aristotle, says Stump, is regularly translated as "essence"; it "seems to be the same criterion as Boethius's 'predicated of the substance' *(substantialiter, or de substantia praedicabitur)*."

89. "Diffinitio vero est oratio quae uniuscujusque rei quidem esse designat." *TD*, p. 64 (PL 64 1196C). See Stump's note 10, p. 129.

sesses an act of being equivalent to goodness, and this allowed for Aquinas's very real advance. Still, we hold that Aquinas attributed to Boethius, to the largest extent possible, his, Aquinas's, own views.

Today an exegete would strive not to "read into" another author one's own views. Such, however, was not Aquinas's attitude. Although we do not know his mind, one can construct a possible viewpoint based on what he actually did. This was to offer a solution he considered correct to an important philosophical problem in the context of another's work and, moreover, to attribute to that author, Boethius, a solution incipient in that author's thought and one which his language would bear. Boethius *does* associate coming-to-be, and therefore actually existing, with goodness, and he does use the term *esse* as a principle of being. The overriding intention of Aquinas seems clear: to arrive at truth; in the process, he wants to give to another—to one who was surely an inspiration for him—maximum credit. We shall cite a few other passages on which Aquinas confers an interpretation more developed than the view of the author he was expounding; in all of these, the process worked to the reinterpreted author's credit, at least according to Aquinas's teaching.

As has been seen, Boethius says that forms cannot be substrates; matter is required for accidents. In the *De trinitate* (2, ll. 40–55) Boethius says that God cannot be a substrate, because He is a pure form, and forms cannot be substrates. Accidents in, for example, human beings are accounted for by the presence of matter. Boethius thus notes a similarity between God and embodied forms: Neither, strictly speaking, is the subject of accidents. Aquinas affirms this in two passages. In *ST* 1.29.2 ad 5 he says, "The individual composed of matter and form substands in relation to accident from the nature of matter *(ex proprietate materiae).* Hence Boethius says *(De trinitate):* 'A simple form cannot be a subject.'"[90] In *ST* 1.54.3 ad 2 Aquinas holds that God as Pure Act cannot be a subject of accidents and Boethius was referring to God when he denied that forms can be substrates. So far Aquinas seems to have represented Boethius's views on form accurately. But further examination of the latter passage

---

90. ". . . individuum compositum ex materia et forma, habet quod substet accidenti, ex proprietate materiae. Unde et Boetius dicit, in libro *de Trin.: forma simplex subiectum esse non potest.*"

shows that Aquinas contrasts God as Pure *Act* to angels as pure *forms;* the latter, for Aquinas, *can* have accidents. The Angelic Doctor's reference to Boethius in this context suggests that Boethius himself affirmed the distinction between Pure Act and merely pure forms. But Boethius does not, and could not, embrace such a position; as already noted, he has no metaphysical basis for it.

Again, in the first argument to the contrary in *Summa theologiae* 1.5.1 Thomas cites Boethius as saying that in nature *(in rebus)* it is one fact that things are good, it is another fact that they are, or exist. In his response Aquinas does not note that Boethius says that this would be the case *if there were no God.* What St. Thomas does is use the preliminary argument as a springboard to launch his detailed analysis of the correlations of kinds of being and kinds of goodness. Recall that for Aquinas being good absolutely *(simpliciter)* corresponds to being relatively (the actuality of accidents); being good relatively *(secundum quid)* corresponds to being absolutely (substantial being). The difference between being and being good to which Boethius alludes is, says St. Thomas, to be referred to being good absolutely, and being absolutely, which according to Aquinas do not correspond. It is true that, since in the place cited Boethius is speaking about what would be the case if there were no God, and since according to this impossible hypothesis creatures would be good only accidentally, Boethius *is* distinguishing between the essential and the accidental realms. But Aquinas's explication of kinds of goodness corresponding to kinds of being is not found in Boethius. Indeed, in his *De hebdomadibus* Boethius's primary concern is with the goodness that belongs to a creature by virtue of its fundamental principle of being. But again, for Aquinas this is not goodness in an absolute or proper sense. Thus Aquinas draws on a statement Boethius considers counterfactual in order to represent a doctrine he, St. Thomas, develops and embraces. But again, Aquinas in no way demeans his predecessor; rather, he credits him with a teaching which may in some sense appear literally in his writings but which clearly goes beyond his intent.

The sort of interpretation we have been illustrating is traditionally termed "pious interpretation," and in other passages Aquinas himself uses language similar to this. For example, he contends that the proposition "The Father alone is God" is false, since the usual way of under-

standing it would be that it implies that neither the Son, nor the Holy Spirit, is also God. He discusses possible ways of reading it that would make it true, but concludes that these do not hold up grammatically. "Hence," he says, "a way of speaking such as this <'The Father alone is God'> is not to be stretched but rather to be explained piously *(pie expo-nenda)* should it be found anywhere in authoritative writing."[91]

Boethius and Fundamental Goodness

Boethius did not articulate a *ratio* of fundamental goodness. Still, a discussion of interpretation might be the appropriate introduction to an attempt to supply the crucial notion. This is not to claim that Boethius explicitly held the following view; we offer it as a possible answer to one asking whether and how Boethius could satisfactorily respond to the question of what fundamental goodness might be.

Let us here recall Boethius's claims (1) that we can think of creatures or finite beings as if they were not from God, although *in fact* they must be created by Him, and (2) if finite beings were not from God they might be accidentally good, but they would not be substantially good, or good insofar as they are. From this it is clear that for Boethius fundamental goodness must be a character or property dependent upon a creature's actually having been created by God. But what property different from accidental goodness is such that it is grounded in a dependence relation on God, but need not be *thought of* as characterizing finite beings (inasmuch as these can be thought of as existing yet not from God, and hence lacking fundamental goodness)?

The difficulty of this question might be mitigated by attempting to locate some general notion of goodness in Boethius. In his work on the *Topics* of Cicero, Boethius discusses maximal propositions: fundamental universal propositions for which there is no proof, the truth of which is known *per se*, and which provide the ground for the truth of other kinds of propositions.[92] In considering the maximal proposition "many goods

---

91. "Unde non est extendenda talis locutio; sed pie exponenda, sicubi inveniatur in authentica scriptura." *ST* 1.31.4. On pious interpretation, see also 1.36.4 ad 7; 1.39.5 ad 1; 1.40.4 ad 1; 1.43.2 ad 1; 3.4.3 ad 1; and *Scriptum super Sententiarum librum I*, d. 5, q. 1, a. 2.

92. *ICT*, p. 33 (PL 64 1051); *TD*, p. 33 (PL 64 1176C), p. 46 (PL 64 1185A); see also Stump's note 23, p. 113, and pp. 180–82.

are preferred to fewer," Boethius notes that this is true of things in the same genus, but there are other considerations. In the course of explaining these, he states "Also, what is unimpaired is judged better than what is corrupted; for things that are unimpaired preserve their form, but things that are corrupted and damaged in some part lose whatever excellence of form they had."[93] Again

> . . . things that are completely developed are naturally superior to things that are not completely developed, for those that are completely developed have attained their form, but those that are not completely developed have not. Also we think that wholes are in the same way superior to parts, for what is a whole has the form appropriate to its nature, but what is a part and depends on the complete development of the whole has not yet received the form of its excellence (unless it is referred to the completed whole).[94]

These passages suggest that before Aquinas, Boethius, not unlike Aristotle, associated completeness and goodness. Yet, as noted above, for Aquinas the completeness that is goodness is identical in reality with being. Our claim, however, is that Boethius had no distinct principle of *esse* that he could consider identical with goodness. One might then wonder whether Boethius did not deem goodness simply to be development. If so, would this goodness be accidental or fundamental? Surely not the latter, inasmuch as one could hardly think of things as existing and yet not to some degree developed. Yet Boethius claims that one can think of an item as existing yet not fundamentally good: If it were not from God, it would merely be accidentally good.

Still, development is a type of completeness; this latter may well have a wider *ratio* that could encompass fundamental goodness. Indeed, if

93. "Integra etiam potius quam contaminata melioris rei judicium ferunt. Nam quae integra sunt, suam speciem servant, quae contaminata sunt atque ex aliqua parte vitiata, si qua etiam inerat, speciei pulchritudinem perdiderunt." *ICT,* p. 173 (PL 64 1161).

94. "Perfecta . . . imperfectis naturaliter excellunt, illa enim suam formam adepta sunt, illa minime. Tota etiam partibus eodem modo excellentiora esse arbitramur: nam quod totum est, habet naturae propriam formam. Quod vera pars est et ad totius nititur perfectionem, nondum suae pulchritudinis speciem cepit, nisi ad totius integritatem referatur." *ICT,* p. 174 (PL 64 1161). Cf. Augustine, *De libero arbitrio* 2.20.203 (CSEL 74, ed. W.M. Green [Vienna: 1956], p. 88, ll. 5–7).

one considers something that is complete simply to be something that is as it is supposed to be, that has what belongs to it, various possibilities of what fundamental goodness might be suggest themselves.[95] Perhaps such goodness might be the relation of depending for existence on God?[96] This relation may be thought to belong to a creature as a creature, yet we need not think of such dependence when thinking of the finite being. Yet if goodness were *equivalent to* this relation to God, when Boethius says that creatures are fundamentally good *because* of their relation to God he would simply be affirming that "good" is correctly applicable to creatures because they possess that dependence relation, since goodness (even if it is completeness) is constituted by just that relation. This is informative only in the sense that it conveys an appropriate use of the term "good" to one unaware of the identity between goodness and the dependence relation. In this case, no claim is made about a *further* quality or state belonging to a creature owing to, or supervenient upon, that creature's relation to God. Yet consider Boethius's words: ". . . since their being *(esse)* has flowed down from the will of the Good, they are said to be good . . . The second good, . . . because it has flowed from It Whose Being Itself is Good, is itself also good."[97] These

95. In Aquinas, of course, a creature is good relatively, *secundum quid,* just by being: it has its essence joined to its act of being, which "belongs" to it if it is to be at all. It is good absolutely, *simpliciter,* if it has the actuality of its developed potencies.

That Boethius could not have held Aquinas's views on *esse* and goodness also follows from these considerations. Boethius says we can think of finite beings as existing but not fundamentally good, since we can think of them as existing yet not from God. But if the fundamental goodness of a creature were its act of being, we could not think it not fundamentally good, for we could not think of a finite being as existing and yet as not having that which makes it exist.

96. For this view see Scott MacDonald's detailed and careful study "Boethius's Claim That All Substances Are Good," *Archiv für Geschichte der Philosophie* 70.3 (1988), pp. 245–79. In an appendix Prof. MacDonald offers his own translation of Boethius's treatise. MacDonald's argument for goodness as a relational property includes a consideration of passages from the *De trinitate.* We are grateful to Professor MacDonald for sharing his work with us.

97. ". . . quoniam esse eorum a boni uoluntate defluxit bona esse dicuntur . . . Secundum . . . bonum quoniam ex eo fluxit cuius ipsum esse bonum est ipsum quoque bonum est." L.4.B35–39; again, the Latin in Stewart, Rand, and Tester says the same thing.

quotations seem to assert more than an equivalence between goodness and a dependence relation, and more about finite beings than that they are correctly called "good" because they are in that relation. The passages suggest that the finite being acquires something more—goodness—owing to its dependence relation. This relation, then, is the reason for, but not the same as, that goodness.

One might suppose that fundamental goodness is having an orientation toward God. This is in keeping with the Neoplatonist view that all that comes from the One and the Good seeks to return to that Source, a view embraced by Boethius in the *Consolation of Philosophy*.[98] True, when first laying out the problem in the *De hebdomadibus* Boethius does say that everything that is tends to the good. Indeed, he holds that things are good because they seek the good, for, as is stated in the last axiom, everything by nature seeks its like. But again, it does not seem that the claim that things are good because they seek the good is just an assertion that things are appropriately called "good" because they seek the good, since being good *is* seeking the good. Nor does Boethius here seem to be holding that seeking the good *makes* things good. Rather, the fact that things seek the good *reveals* the fact that things are good. What goodness consists in, however, is left unstated.

When one considers Boethius's view of *esse* as discussed above in the light of the notion of completeness, another possibility concerning fundamental goodness arises. Could it not be just the conformity of the embodied form, of the *esse*, to the Form in the mind of God? This would comport with Boethius's claims: Actually existent things are good insofar as they are to the extent that they are from God, and their very *esse* itself is good (L.5.B1–22). The embodied form itself conforms, and because of it the thing conforms to the Form in the divine Mind, but the thing must actually be, and be from God, in order so to conform. This notion harmonizes with Boethius's emphasis on goodness as dependent on the coming-to-be of a creature, already discussed.

Again, Boethius did not actually explicate this view on fundamental

---

98. In Proclus, e.g., see *The Elements of Theology*, 2d ed., tr. E.R. Dodds (Oxford: 1933, rpt. 1971), p. 15, propositions 12 and 13. Chadwick documents the Neoplatonic influence, especially that of Proclus, on Boethius: Chadwick, pp. xiv, 20–21, 129. In *Con.* see, e.g., 3, m. 2, and 9; 4, m. 6.

goodness. But we offer it as a plausible interpretation, because it indicates a type of profound completeness for a creature to have based on its relation to God: To the extent that it is, it is what it is supposed to be, or has what belongs to it, or is complete, according to the Form in God's mind. Moreover, one can think of a creature without thinking of its conforming to God's Mind, even though, for Boethius, in fact it must so conform just because it is from God. And if it did exist and were not from God (the impossible hypothesis), it could not have this conformity, since it is the relation of image to archetype.[99]

Aquinas on Boethius
Being

Above it was noted that Aquinas attributes to Boethius his, Aquinas's, notion of "being." This claim will here be substantiated, and we shall offer highlights of Aquinas's explanation and interpretation of Boethius in this regard.

What is striking to the careful reader is how much Aquinas stresses form as a principle of being, reminiscent of the statement made by Boethius in the *De trinitate* that all being *(esse)* is from form. One could agree that in Aquinas this characterizing of form as a principle of being affirms the distinction between the two. But it does not suggest the metaphysical priority Aquinas enunciates elsewhere, for example, in this passage from the *Summa theologiae:* "Being naturally results *(esse per se consequitur)* from the form of a creature given the influence of God, just as light results from the diaphanous nature of the air, given the influence of the sun."[100] The air conveys the light, as the form structures

---

99. This is not the place to discuss the notion of goodness in the *Consolation*. It might be noted, however, that in this work goodness and completeness are associated (e.g., 3, pr. 10). Of course the tie to completion here is primarily concerned with virtue as the completing aspect of humans, and happiness as our ultimate completion (3, pr. 2, m. 2, pr. 10, pr. 12; *Con.* 4, pr. 2 and pr. 6). This is the type of completion Aquinas would characterize as in the accidental realm.

Many of the points made in this section were presented in "Boethius: Two Works, One Goodness?" by Janice Schultz, *Proceedings of the PMR Conference* 18 (1993–94), pp. 121–32. The article starts at the fourth paragraph on p. 121; the first three paragraphs on that page, which belong to the previous article in the volume, were mistakenly reprinted.

100. ". . . esse per se consequitur formam creaturae, supposito tamen influxu

the being. It is not a question of the one efficiently causing the other. Yet let us compare passages from the *Exposition:*

> . . . since form is a principle of being *(essendi),* according to any form possessed, something is said in some way to possess 'to be' *(esse).* If, therefore, that form is not outside the essence of that which possesses it, but constitutes that item's essence, from the fact that the item possesses such a form it will be said to have being *(esse)* without qualification . . .[101]

And again, ". . . when something is said to be 'in this, that it is,' *substance is signified,* because the form making this reality to be constitutes its essence *(essenciam)."*[102] To be sure, similar passages can be found in the mature *Summa theologiae,*[103] but there the metaphysical priority noted above is made with utmost clarity.

Subtle parallels and turns of phrase by Aquinas also reveal a linguistic accommodation to an emphasis on the importance of form, thereby underscoring his philosophical kinship with his predecessor. For example, when in the *Exposition* Aquinas discusses Boethius's claim that *esse* does not possess anything outside itself as an admixture, Thomas argues that *forms,* as examples of abstract things that he had earlier categorized as such with being,[104] do not possess anything outside themselves, concluding that being itself *(ipsum esse)* has nothing outside its own *essence (essenciam)* as an admixture (L.2.A114–146).

Aquinas thus speaks, somewhat uncharacteristically, about the "essence of being." He also speaks of the being belonging to essence, or "essential being," for example, when he says that absolute goodness, or goodness *simpliciter,* does not belong to created goods according to their essential being *(ipsum esse essenciale eorum),* but according to something

---

Dei: sicut lumen sequitur diaphanum aeris, supposito influxu solis." *ST* 1.104.1 ad 1.

101. ". . . quia . . . forma est principium essendi, necesse est quod secundum quamlibet formam habitam habens aliqualiter esse dicatur. Si ergo forma illa non sit preter essenciam habentis, set constituat eius essenciam, ex eo quod habet talem formam dicetur habens esse simpliciter . . . ," L.2.A156–161.

102. ". . . cum dicitur aliquid esse in eo quod est, *significatur substancia,* quia scilicet forma faciens hoc esse constituit essenciam rei." L.2.A175–178.

103. E.g., *ST* 1.5.5 ad 3; 1.6.3; 1.17.3; 1.45.5 ad 1; 1.50.5; 1.65.4; 1.77.1 ad 3.

104. L.2.A43–44; 89–97, although here Aquinas distinguishes forms and *esse,* in that the latter can participate in nothing, since it is most common.

superadded, i.e., their virtue.[105] This view on goodness is the one we have seen articulated in the *Summa theologiae*. Recall that the type of goodness that is the completion of the potentialities of a creature—goodness absolutely or properly speaking—is not present simply as the fundamental act of being that makes something to be, i.e., the being that actualizes essence. Rather, goodness properly speaking pertains to further actualization. Now when Boethius claims that goodness pertains to essence *(essenciam)*, Aquinas explains such a reference by pointing out that each reality is termed 'good' in accord with the *completion* of its nature or essence (L.5.A86–92, our emphasis). That is, Aquinas uses Boethius's reference to essence to suggest his, Aquinas's, doctrine of goodness as *being*: Goodness is the fullness of being, the *completion* or *actualization*, of nature. Boethius, however, uses "essence" in the place cited to refer to just that metaphysical principle of a thing that makes it *what* it is, and to contrast simply be-ing with acting in finite things.[106] Aquinas certainly has moved metaphysically beyond Boethius here, but he maintains an emphasis on essence as the complementary principle to *esse*, being.

Complementariness of principles implies a distinction, and, despite

---

105. L.4.A150–160. Aquinas's use of the phrase "essential being," *esse essenciale*, suggests that the "something superadded" is another kind of being or actuality.

In *Summa contra gentiles (SCG)* 3.20 Aquinas claims that the form of a composite being is of itself good, because through it the substance actually is. In *ST* he also says that a form is good in that through it something has being or actuality: e.g., 1.48.3. But forms alone do not have goodness, so that mathematical entities, having no real being, have no goodness: 1.5.3 ad 4; and only God is good essentially, or by essence: 1.6.3. In *SCG* 3.20 Aquinas takes the position that goodness in one sense may be said to extend further than being, in that matter, as potential being, seeks being, and thus may be called good without qualification; good, then, is of a wider scope than being. Aquinas revises this view in *ST* 1.5.3 ad 3; see also 1.48.3.

106. Aquinas also points out that God is the very *Essence* of Goodness: L.5.A88–89.

It might be noted here that in his *De hebdomadibus* Boethius has little concern with the type of goodness that for Aquinas is the completion of nature; recall, for Boethius creatures could be good merely by accidental participation if God did *not* exist. In the next section we shall discuss further Aquinas's treatment of goodness in the *Exposition*.

his stress on form, in the *Exposition* Aquinas unquestionably articulates the distinction between essence and *esse*. It is clear from the outset that one way he uses *esse* is to mean "act of being," although he continues to employ *id quod est* generally to indicate "concrete being." "To be *(esse)*" signifies abstractly, as does "to run"; *id quod est* signifies concretely, and is the subject of being *(essendi)* as "that which runs" is the subject of running. Rather than speaking of participation in the form of being *(forma essendi)* as does Boethius, Aquinas states that the concrete being participates in the act of being *(actus essendi)*. As in the *Summa theologiae*, his point is that *esse* or being is that whereby a substance is, as running *(cursus)* is that whereby a runner runs.[107] Something is, then, because it participates in *ipsum esse*.[108] But because *esse* is most common, it cannot participate in anything (L.2.A95–97). On the other hand, whiteness, a form, can participate in color (L.2.A93–95).

When employing *esse* as just explained, Aquinas attributes this usage to Boethius. For example, after noting that that which is participates in the act of being, Aquinas says,

> And this is what he <Boethius> says: That *being itself as yet is not*, because to be is not attributed to 'to be' itself as the subject of being, but that *which is . . . the form of being . . . taken on*, namely, by receiving the very act of being, *is and stands together*, that is, it subsists in itself.[109]

Again, when the Angelic Doctor contrasts *esse*, which can participate in nothing else, with a form such as whiteness, which can participate in color, Thomas continues, "Therefore this is what he <Boethius> says,

107. L.2.A39–59; cf. *ST* 1.50.2 ad 3. In the latter passage Aquinas describes the twofold composition of material beings, and the composition of angels as that of nature and *esse*. He also refers to Boethius, claiming he distinguishes between *esse* and what is, *quod est*. Aquinas then says: "For what-is is the form itself subsisting; the being itself however is that by which the substance is, as the running is that by which the runner runs (. . . nam quod est est ipsa forma subsistens; ipsum autem esse est quo substantia est, sicut cursus est quo currens currit . . .)."

108. L.2.A95–112; 191–195.

109. "Et hoc est quod dicit quod *ipsum esse nondum est* quia non attribuitur sibi esse sicut subiecto essendi, set id *quod est, accepta essendi forma*, scilicet suscipiendo ipsum actum essendi, *est atque consistit*, id est in se ipso subsistit." L.2.A59–63.

that *what-is,* namely being *(ens), can participate in something; but being itself (ipsum esse) in no way participates in anything.*"[110]

Moreover, in his discussion of levels of composite beings, Aquinas explicitly ascribes to Boethius an articulation of the real distinction between *esse* as act of being and the concrete item. Aquinas prepares for his treatment of simple and composite beings by going beyond the text of Boethius in asserting that the diversity of *id quod est* and *esse* is initially to be taken as referring to intentions rather than things (L.2.A36–39; 196–201). He can then say "just as 'to be' *(esse)* and 'what is' *(quod est)* differ according to intention, so in composite items they differ in reality *(realiter)*".[111] In this context Aquinas refers to Boethius thus: ". . . therefore a composite reality is not its own 'to be' *(esse);* and so he [Boethius] says that in *every composite it is one thing* to be a being *(esse ens),* and *another* to be the composite itself, which IS by participating in *being itself (ipsum esse).*"[112] Of course for Aquinas composite beings encompass not only creatures composed of matter and form, but also subsistent created forms. For in these latter there is still a distinction of *esse* and essence: "Nevertheless, because every <such> form you like is determinative of 'to be' itself *(ipsius esse),* not one of them is 'to be' itself, but rather is what possesses 'to be.'"[113]

One alternative to holding that Aquinas attributed to Boethius a position that the latter did not embrace is to propose that Aquinas really did think that by *esse* Boethius meant "act of being." Of course, if our in-

---

110. "Hoc est ergo quod dicit quod id *quod est,* scilicet ens, *participare aliquo potest; set ipsum esse nullo modo participat aliquo* . . . ," L.2.A102–105.

111. ". . . sicut esse et quod est differunt secundum intentiones, ita in compositis differunt realiter." L.2.A204–206.

112. ". . . res ergo composita non est suum esse; et ideo dicit quod in *omni composito aliud est* esse ens et *aliud* ipsum compositum quod est participando *ipsum esse.*" L.2.A212–215. Boethius does not use *ens.* The language of Aquinas here, as presented in the Leonine edition, is not as lucid as it usually is. According to this language, he may be interpreted as saying that it is one thing to be something from the point of view of act of to be, and another thing to be a composite thing from the point of view of essence. But perhaps Aquinas did not add the *ens;* see note 10 to the translation below.

113. "Quia tamen quelibet forma est determinatiua ipsius esse, nulla earum est ipsum esse, set est habens esse . . . ," L.2.A234–236. Aquinas does not use the example of angels but rather speaks of Platonic forms.

terpretation of Boethius is correct, this view of Aquinas would cast a negative light on his intelligence, whereas holding that Thomas engaged in pious interpretation would in no way impugn his character. Furthermore, passages already cited suggest that Aquinas could not have overlooked Boethius's stance. As noted above, when Aquinas comments on the passage in which Boethius says that what, or that which *(id quod)* things are they possess from that which is being *(ex eo quod est esse)*, Thomas drops the term *id*, so that "that which" becomes "that": "But that certain things might 'be,' this *they possess from that which is being*" (L.3.A108–109). Is one to suppose that Aquinas did not notice the *id* in Boethius's formulation? But, as always, Aquinas's shift is done gently, while granting Boethius maximum credit.

Consider, too, that when discussing simple and composite beings Aquinas does not mention angels as subsistent forms, but uses the example of Platonic forms, which for Aquinas are not subsistent at all! Could this be at least in part owing to the fact that the mention of angels might raise the question of why Boethius offers no metaphysical analysis of them (which, of course, he cannot, at least on the view that he holds *esse* to be form)? Might not Aquinas's omission here intimate that he was aware of the deficiency in Boethius's theory, a deficiency the Angelic Doctor was remedying through pious interpretation?

Goodness

As has been seen, in the section of the *De hebdomadibus* after the axioms Boethius identifies "good by participation" and "accidentally good"; he claims that only accidental goodness could accrue to a finite being if it were not from God. These points suggest that for Boethius creatures are not by participation good insofar as they are. Indeed, nowhere in the *De hebdomadibus* does Boethius *state* that in fact finite beings are, in any way, good by participation. Now on our interpretation finite beings do, according to Boethius, participate in their forms, which become good in creation. True, this is not participation in goodness, but in something good. Still, it involves a type of participation more basic than that associated with possession of accidents. If, however, Boethius understood this participation as a kind of mediated "good by participation," he left it to his readers to make this understanding explicit.

Above it was explained that for Aquinas being and goodness are the same in reality; thus for him creatures both are, and are good, by participation, because just as they participate in being *(esse)*, so they participate in goodness. But not unlike Boethius on participation, here Aquinas does not present his doctrine full blown. In this exposition he does clearly contend that creatures participate in an *actus essendi* in order to be (L.2.A54–63), but he *suggests*, rather than declares, the identity of goodness and being,[114] and there is no pious interpretation of Boethius where there are no words of his to bear it. It would seem to follow that St. Thomas would avoid actually saying in the *Exposition* that creatures participate in goodness, and this in fact is the case, despite his somewhat elaborate discussion of participation.

On the other hand, in the *Summa theologiae* Thomas's teaching is clear: Creatures are good by participation.[115] Aquinas explicitly holds that if something is not, for example, a being, or good, or just by essence and yet is a being, or is good, or just, it must be this way by participation.[116] This is because creatures are not identical with their essences, a position Boethius also holds. But this position helps form the foundation for setting out the dilemma of the *De hebdomadibus,* and Boethius must imply a mediated participation in goodness, *via* the form or essence, to allow for a non-accidental, profound way that creatures can be good without being Goodness Itself.[117] In contrast, as we have seen, Aquinas's participation is in *esse* which *is* goodness, albeit a limited and created goodness. To understand the difference between Boethius's and

114. In L.4.A145–160 Aquinas speaks of a creature's being absolutely good insofar as it is complete in *esse* and operation, thus correlating goodness in the proper sense with *esse.*

115. *ST* 1.6.3, including *sed contra; ST* 1–2.34.3 ad 2; see also *ST* 1.6.4; 1.47.1; 1.103.4, 2–2.26.2 ad 3 and next note. Aquinas makes reference to the *De hebdomadibus* in 1.6.3 where he cites Boethius as saying all things but God are good by participation *(sed contra).* As has been noted, Boethius does not affirm this to be the case in that treatise, although he does in other works, such as the *Consolation:* 3, pr. 11.

116. See also *ST* 1.44.1; 1.3.4; 1.4.3 ad 3; 1.61.1.

117. Recall that in axioms 1 (II) and 5 (VI) Boethius allows for participation by a thing in *esse,* or form. Cf. *ST* 1.45.5 ad 1. In the *Exposition* Aquinas notes that in the section of the *De hebdomadibus* following the axioms, Boethius means by "participation" that by which a subject participates in an accident: L.3.A63–65.

Aquinas's accounts of participation to explain how creatures can be good insofar as they are is to understand the fundamental differences between Boethius and Aquinas on the relation of *esse* and goodness.

Both through pious interpretation and by his silence on some points in the *Exposition* Aquinas minimizes these differences. Indeed, toward the end of the work Aquinas intimates that Boethius's solution is compatible with his own:

> His <Boethius's> solution comes back to this, therefore, that the Being of the First is good according to Its own intelligible structure because the Nature and Essence of the First Good is nothing other than Goodness. The being of a secondary good is good indeed, not according to the intelligible structure of its own essence—because its essence is not Goodness Itself . . . but its <the secondary good's> own being *(esse)* possesses this, that it is good owing to a relation to the First Good . . .[118]

Aquinas then identifies this *esse* or being as the type he calls "substantial" (or in this work "essential") rather than "accidental." He does not, however, here *equate* being and goodness, nor does he claim that Boethius equates these, despite the fact that he presents him as profoundly *associating* them.

Above it was pointed out that, despite Boethius's lack of the identification of the principle of *esse* as an act of being, he nevertheless stresses that the essence of a creature becomes good only in the process of creation, the coming-to-*be* of something. According to a possible interpretation proffered above, this is to say that goodness is constituted by an actual conformity between the existing embodied essence and the essence as it is in God's mind. Whether or not this interpretation be correct, it remains that, although Boethius does not hold that goodness is *esse* itself, for him, as for Aquinas, only actually existing things are good. And though Aquinas emphasizes the coextensivity of goodness and being, he, like Boethius, affirms its relational aspect:

---

118. "Redit ergo eius solutio ad hoc quod esse primi est secundum propriam rationem bonum, quia natura et essencia primi boni nichil aliud est quam bonitas; esse autem secundi boni est quidem bonum, non secundum rationem proprie essencie quia essencia eius non est ipsa bonitas . . . set esse eius habet quod sit bonum ex habitudine ad primum bonum . . . ," L.4.A132–140.

Now perfection in a thing is threefold: first, according to the constitution of its own being *(esse)*; second, with respect to any accidents added as necessary for its complete operation; third, perfection consists in *attaining something else as an end.*[119]

For Boethius the central relational aspect is dependence on God; for him, as well as for Aquinas, such origin and dependence are necessarily correlated with seeking Him, the Source of all creation.

Editorial Policies

This English translation of the *Expositio libri De hebdomadibus* by Saint Thomas Aquinas is based on the Latin text provided by the Leonine editors in the fiftieth volume of their critical edition of all the works by Aquinas.[120] Undertaken at the behest of Pope Leo XIII, and hence termed "the Leonine edition," the first volume appeared in 1882; the Latin title of the series is *Sancti Thomae de Aquino, Opera omnia, iussu Leonis XIII P.M. edita.* Tome 50, in which the work here translated appears, has been published at Rome: Commissio Leonina and at Paris: Editions du Cerf, 1992; the editors responsible for this work are Louis J. Bataillon and the late Carlo A. Grassi. The same volume presents the text of the only other Boethian work as handled by Aquinas, *Super Boetium de trinitate*, edited by Pierre-M. J. Gils.

In the Leonine edition, the Latin text of Saint Thomas's *Exposition of the Book On the Hebdomads* is divided into five sections, each headed by a Roman numeral. The relatively short Boethian text with which each section opens carries an Arabic numeral in the margin at every fifth line. The Arabic numerals begin a new series at the Thomistic text which undertakes the explanation of that section of the Boethian work; again,

---

119. "Perfectio autem alicuius rei triplex est. Prima quidem, secundum quod in suo esse constituitur. Secunda vero, prout ei aliqua accidentia superadduntur, ad suam perfectam operationem necessaria. Tertia vero perfectio alicuius est per hoc, quod aliquid aliud attingit sicut finem." *ST* 1.6.3, our emphasis; see also 1.6.4.

120. The Leonine text has been slightly altered at four points in Aquinas's commentary: in Chapter 2, line 279, the comma has been moved from before to after *est;* in Chapter 3, line 63, *substantialiter* has been changed to *substancialiter* to conform with spelling elsewhere; in Chapter 3, line 91, *par* has been changed to *per;* and in Chapter 5, line 100, *quot* has been changed to *quod.*

the numerals occur in the margin at every fifth line. The Leonine line numbers for both the Boethian and the Thomistic texts are indicated in the Latin text and, as precisely as possible, in the English translation below, but only every tenth line is numbered, and the numerals appear in the text itself, not in the margin. Our abbreviation for the Leonine text specifies the work (L), section (1–5), author, and line numbers; hence L.1.A40–50 indicates the first section between line numbers 40 and 50 of Aquinas's commentary; L.2.B10–20 indicates the second section between line numbers 10–20 of the Boethian text contained in the *Exposition*. In the English translation we use "Chapter" to designate each section.

It must be kept in mind that Aquinas expounded the manuscript text at his disposal, not a modern critical edition. The Boethian text in this work is not identical with that used in the Stewart, Rand, and Tester translation, listed in the bibliography. It is, however, not significantly different, and inasmuch as the Stewart, Rand, and Tester work is readily available, we did not think it necessary generally to point out textual differences. Biblical references in Aquinas's text are to the Vulgate.

In each chapter below, the English text of Boethius is in italics. Italicized words in the Leonine text of Aquinas that indicate his references to Boethius's words are also italicized in our translation. These may not be the exact words of Boethius; we translate what Aquinas actually wrote, according to this edition. Where the words of Aquinas are those of Boethius, we translate identically. Ellipses (. . .) are inserted in these italicized phrases where deemed appropriate. Double quotation marks are used in the translation itself wherever these appear in the Latin text; single quotation marks are used at our discretion. We use angle brackets both for our insertions and where they are used in the Leonine edition.

Because of our understanding of Boethius's metaphysical views, when he uses *esse* as a substantive we translate it only as "being." When translating Aquinas's own words, however, *esse* is rendered as "being" or as "to be," depending on context. When Aquinas uses *ens,* we translate it as "being" or "a being," again depending on context.

An Exposition of the
On the Hebdomads
of Boethius

Postulas ut ex ebdomadibus nostris eius questionis obscuritatem que continet modum quo substantie in eo quod sint bone sint cum non sint substantialia bona digeram et paulo euidentius monstrem.

Idque eo dicis esse faciendum quod non sit omnibus notum iter huiusmodi scriptionum. Tuus uero testis ipse sum quam hec uiuaciter fueris ante complexus.

Ebdomadas uero ego michi ipse commentor, potius que ad memoriam meam speculata conseruo quam {10} cuiquam participo quorum lasciuia ac petulancia nichil a ioco risuque patitur esse coniunctum.

Pro hinc tu ne sis obscuritatibus breuitatis aduersus que cum sint archani fida custodia tum id habent commodi quod cum hiis solis qui digni sunt colloquntur.

Vt igitur in mathematica fieri solet ceterisque etiam disciplinis preposui terminos regulasque quibus cuncta que sequntur efficiam.

Communis animi conceptio est enuntiatio quam quisque probat auditam.

{20} Harum duplex est modus. Nam una ita communis est ut omnium sit hominum ueluti si hanc proponas: si duobus equalibus equalia auferas que relinquntur equalia esse, nullus id intelligens neget. Alia uero est doctorum tantum, que tamen ex talibus communis animi conceptionibus uenit ut est: que incorporalia sunt in loco non esse; et cetera que non uulgus set docti comprobant.

EXPOSITIO

Precurre prior in domum tuam, et illic aduocare, et illic lude et age conceptiones tuas, Ecclesiastici XXXII.

Habet hoc priuilegium sapiencie studium quod operi suo prosequendo magis ipsa sibi sufficiat. In exterioribus enim operibus Indiget homo plurimorum auxilio, set in contemplatione sapiencie tanto aliquis efficacius operatur quanto magis solitarius secum commoratur. Et ideo

CHAPTER 1

You request of me that I set out in order from my hebdomads the obscure
question which deals with the way in which substances are good insofar as they
are,[1] *although they are not substantial goods, and that I show this in a fairly*
clear way.

You also say that this ought to be done so that the method of writings of this
sort not be familiar to all.[2] *I myself am your witness to how eagerly you have al-*
ready wrestled with these matters.

Still, I myself have the hebdomads in my mind and prefer to keep those specu-
lations in my memory rather than {10} share them with anyone whose wanton-
ness and petulance tolerate nothing that has not been linked to joke and laugh-
ter!

In accord with this, may you not be adverse to the obscurities of brevity, since
those obscurities are the faithful defense of secret teaching, and they have the ad-
vantage that they speak only to those who are worthy.

Therefore, as customarily happens in mathematics and in other disciplines as
well, I have set out first the terms and rules by which I shall develop all that fol-
lows:

A common conception of the mind is a statement that everyone approves on
hearing.

{20} There are two sorts of these. One sort is common in that it belongs to all
humans, so that should you propose this, 'If from two equals you subtract equals,
what remain are equals,' no one understanding this would deny it. The other
sort, however, belongs only to the learned, even though it comes from such concep-
tions of our common mind, as in this case: 'Things that are incorporeal are not in
a place,' and others, which the learned but not the common crowd approve.

EXPOSITION

First run into your own house, and there call them in, and there play and
work out your conceptions, Ecclesiasticus XXXII <15–16>.

Striving for Wisdom possesses this peculiar advantage: In doing her
work she is more than sufficient to herself. For in exterior works a human being needs much help, but in the contemplation of Wisdom the
more one remains solitary and alone with oneself, the more efficacious-

3

sapiens in uerbis propositis hominem ad se ipsum reuocat {10} dicens: *Precurre prior in domum tuam*, id est ad mentem tuam ab exterioribus sollicite redeas antequam ab alio occupetur per cuius sollicitudinem distrahatur; unde dicitur Sap. VIII: "Intrans in domum meam conquiescam cum illa", scilicet cum sapiencia. Sicut autem requiritur ad contemplationem sapiencie quod mentem suam aliquis preoccupet ut totam domum suam contemplatione sapiencie impleat, ita etiam requiritur quod ipse totus per intentionem interius assit, ne scilicet {20} eius intentio ad diuersa trahatur, et ideo subdit: *et illic aduocare*, id est totam intentionem tuam ibi congrega. Sic igitur interiori domo totaliter uacuata et homine totaliter per intentionem in ea existente, quid agendum sit exponit, subdens: *et illic lude*. Vbi considerandum est quod sapiencie contemplatio conuenienter ludo comparatur propter duo que est in ludo inuenire. Primo quidem quia ludus delectabilis est et contemplatio sapiencie maximam habet delectationem, unde Eccli. {30} XXIIII dicitur ex ore Sapiencie: "Spiritus meus super mel dulcis". Secundo quia operationes ludi non ordinantur ad aliud set propter se queruntur, et hoc idem competit in delectationibus sapiencie. Contingit enim quandoque quod aliquis apud se ipsum delectatur consideratione eorum que concupiscit uel que agere proponit, set hec delectatio ordinatur ad aliquid exterius ad quod nititur peruenire; quod si deficiat uel tardetur delectationi huiusmodi adiungitur non minor afflictio, secundum {40} illud Eccli. XXXIII: "Risus dolore miscebitur". Set delectatio contemplationis sapiencie in se ipsa habet delectationis causam, unde nullam anxietatem patitur quasi expectans aliquid quod desit; propter quod dicitur Sap. VIII: "Non habet amaritudinem conuersatio nec tedium conuictus illius", scilicet sapiencie. Et ideo diuina Sapiencia suam delectationem ludo comparat, Prou. VIII: "Delectabar per singulos dies ludens coram eo", ut per diuersos dies diuersarum ueritatum considerationes {50} intelligantur. Vnde et hic subditur: *et illic age conceptiones tuas*, per quas scilicet homo cognitionem accipit ueritatis.

ly one works. And therefore, in the words proposed, the Wise Man calls one back to oneself {10} saying: *First run into your own house;* that is, away from external things you should, with solicitude, retire to your own mind, before it is occupied by what is alien and, through concern for that, is distracted. Hence it is said in Wisdom VIII <16>: "Entering into my house I shall take my rest with her," namely, with Wisdom. Just as the contemplation of Wisdom requires taking possession of one's own mind beforehand in order to fill one's whole house with the contemplation of Wisdom, so, too, through intention one must be totally within, lest {20} attention be drawn to diverse things. And therefore he adds: *and there call them in,* that is, there gather together your whole attention. Thus, once the interior of the house has been totally emptied, and through attention one is totally present in it, he explains what must be done by adding: *and there play.* Here one must consider that the contemplation of Wisdom is suitably compared to play on two counts, each of which is to be found in play. First, because play is delightful and the contemplation of Wisdom possesses maximum delight, whence Ecclesiasticus {30} XXIIII <27> says by the mouth of Wisdom: "My spirit is sweet above honey." Second, because things done in play are not ordered to anything else, but are sought for their own sake, and this same trait belongs to the delights of Wisdom. For it happens at times that someone is delighted within by considering what one desires, or proposes to do, but this delight is ordered to something external, which one struggles to attain. If there should be a failure or a delay no small affliction is joined to delight of this sort, in accord with {40} the saying of Ecclesiasticus XXXIII <in fact, Proverbs 14:13>: "Laughter is mixed with sorrow." But the delight of contemplating Wisdom has within itself the cause of delight; hence one suffers no anxiety, as if awaiting something that might be lacking. On this account it is said in Wisdom VIII <16>: "Its conversation" (namely that of wisdom) "has no bitterness, nor does dwelling with it have any tedium." And therefore divine Wisdom compares her delight to play, in Proverbs VIII <30>: "I was delighted every day playing before Him," so that through the different 'days' the consideration of different truths {50} might be understood. Hence here is also added: *and there work out your conceptions,* through which, namely, a human being grasps the knowledge of truth.

Huius igitur exortationis sectator Boetius hunc de suis conceptionibus librum nobis edidit qui *de ekdomatibus* dicitur, id est de editionibus,
quia in greco 'ekdidomi' idem est quod edere; in quo quidem libro
Boetius duo facit. Primo enim premittit prohemium. Secundo procedit
ad operis tractatum, ibi: *Diuersum est esse et id quod est* etc.

{60} Circa primum tria facit. Primo ostendit de quo sit intentio.
Secundo quomodo sit tradendum, ibi: *Idque eo dicis esse faciendum* etc.
Tercio tradit ordinem quo procedendum est, ibi: *Vt igitur in mathematica
fieri solet* etc.

Scribit autem hunc librum ad Iohannem dyaconum romane ecclesie
qui ab eo pecierat ut *ex* suis *ekdomatibus,* id est editionibus, dissereret et
exponeret quamdam difficilem questionem per quam soluitur quedam
apparens contrarietas. Dicitur {70} enim quod *substancie* create, in quantum sunt, *bone* sunt, *cum* tamen dicatur quod substancie create *non* sunt
substancialia bona. Set hoc dicitur solius Dei proprium esse: quod enim
conuenit alicui in quantum est uidetur ei substancialiter conuenire. Et
ideo si substancie create in quantum sunt bone sunt, consequens uidetur quod sint substancialia bona.

Deinde cum dicit: *Idque eo dicis* etc., ostendit per quem modum hoc
tradere uult, id est non {80} plane set obscure; et circa hoc tria facit.
Primo ostendit quod intendit obscure dicere. Secundo ostendit hunc
modum esse sibi consuetum, ibi: *Ekdomatas uero* etc. Tercio concludit
quod hic modus debeat ei esse acceptus, ibi: *Pro hinc tu* etc.

Dicit ergo primo quod ille ad quem scribit hoc ita petebat predicta
esse facienda, quia uia eorum que hic scribenda sunt *non* esset *omnibus*
nota qui non eodem desiderio ad hoc afficiebantur quo ipse, cui Boetius
testimonium perhibet quod predicta {90} fuerat *uiuaciter ante complexus,*
id est uel perspicaciter intelligendo uel feruenter desiderando.

Deinde cum dicit: *Ekdomatas uero* etc. ostendit hunc modum etiam

Boethius, therefore, a follower of this exhortation, has edited a book for us concerning his own conceptions, which is called *on the ekdomads,* that is, 'on editions,' because in Greek 'ekdidomi' is the same as 'to edit.' In this book Boethius does two things. First, he sets forth an introduction. Second, he proceeds to what is treated in the work, where he says: *Being and that-which-is are diverse,* etc. <L.2.B1>.

{60} With regard to the first point he does three things. First, he shows what his intention is; second, how that must be treated, where he says: *You also say that this ought to be done so,* etc. Third, he gives the order in which he must proceed, where he says: *Therefore, as customarily happens in mathematics,* etc.

Now he writes this book to John, Deacon of the Roman Church, who had asked that *from* his *ekdomads,* that is, 'editions,' he discuss and explain a certain difficult question through which an apparent contradiction is resolved. For {70} it is said that created *substances,* inasmuch as they are, are *good, although* it is stated, nevertheless, that created substances are *not substantial goods.* But this is said to be a property of God alone, for what belongs to anything inasmuch as it is, seems to belong to it substantially. And, therefore, if created substances are good inasmuch as they are, it seems to follow that they must be substantial goods.

Then when he says: *You also say,* etc., he shows how he wants to convey this, that is, not {80} plainly but obscurely. With regard to this he does three things. First, he shows that he intends to speak obscurely; second, he reveals that this manner is usual with him, where he says: *Still . . . the ekdomads,* etc. Third, he concludes that this manner ought to be acceptable to him <to John the Deacon>, where he says: *In accord with this . . . you,* etc.

Therefore he says first that he to whom he writes this asked that the aforesaid *be* done in this manner, because <then> the way of those things to be written here would *not* be familiar to *all* those not having the same desire for this as he. Boethius gives testimony that {90} he <John> had *eagerly . . . already wrestled* with the aforesaid matters, that is, either by understanding them in a penetrating way, or by fervently desiring to do so.

Then when he <Boethius> says: *Still . . . the hebdomads,* he shows that

sibi esse consuetum, et dicit quod *ipse* solitus erat sibi commentari, id est componere uel excogitare, quasdam *ekdomatas,* id est editiones seu conceptiones, *que pocius* conseruabat ea considerans *ad* sui *memoriam* quam participem eorum faceret aliquem illorum qui propter sui lasciuiam et petulanciam, id est luxuriam {100} et leuitatem, *nichil* aliud *a ioco* et *risu* paciuntur *esse coniunctum,* id est ordinatum uel constructum. Detestantur enim si quis aliquem sermonem coniunxerit aut ordinauerit non ad ludum set ad seria pertinentem.

Deinde cum dicit: *Pro hinc tu* etc., concludit ex premissis quod obscurum sermonem debeat gratanter suscipere, utpote qui talem sermonem ipse pecierat, et hoc est quod dicit *pro hinc,* quia scilicet hoc fecisti ne *iter* nostrarum descriptionum esset {110} omnibus peruium, *ne sis aduersus,* id est contrarius, *obscuritatibus breuitatis,* id est obscuritati presentis libri que est breuitati coniuncta; ex hoc enim quod aliqua breuiter dicuntur magis solent esse obscura. Obscuritas autem cum secretum fideliter custodiat hoc affert utilitatis quod loquitur solum *cum illis qui* digni sunt, id est cum intelligentibus et studiosis qui digni sunt ad secreta sapiencie admitti.

Deinde cum dicit: *Vt igitur in mathematica fieri solet* etc., ostendit quo ordine sit procedendum {120} ut uidelicet per ea que sunt per se nota; et circa hoc duo facit. Primo ponit ordinem procedendi. Secundo notificat illa ex quibus procedere intendit, ibi: *Communis animi conceptio est* etc.

Dicit ergo primo quod ipse intendit primo proponere quedam principia per se nota que uocat *terminos* et *regulas,* terminos quidem quia in huiusmodi principiis stat omnium demonstrationum resolutio, regulas autem quia per ea dirigitur aliquis in cognitione sequencium conclusionum. {130} Ex huiusmodi autem principiis intendit concludere et facere nota omnia que consequenter tractanda sunt, sicut fit in geometria et in aliis demonstratiuis scienciis, que ideo dicuntur discipline quia per eas discipulis aggeneratur sciencia ex demonstratione quam magister proponit.

this manner of writing was also usual for him. He says that *he himself* was accustomed to think over in his own mind, that is, to combine or think out, certain *ekdomads*, that is, 'editions' or 'conceptions.' *Those* he was conserving *in* his *memory rather* than sharing them with some of those people who, owing to wantonness and petulance, that is, luxury {100} and light-headedness, tolerate *nothing* apart from what is *linked to joke* and *laughter,* that is, apart from matters ordered or constructed their way. For they detest it if anyone compose or order any discourse pertaining to serious matters, and not to play.

Then when he says: *In accord with this . . . you,* etc., he concludes from what has been said that obscure discourse ought to be gratefully received, since he <John> himself had requested just such discourse. And this is what he <Boethius> means by *in accord with this,* since, in fact, you <John> have done this lest the *method* of our writings be {110} a passageway for everyone. <Thus> *may you not be adverse,* that is, in opposition to, *the obscurities of brevity,* namely, to the present book's obscurity, which is linked to brevity. For the fact that matters are expressed briefly usually means that they are rather obscure. Still, since obscurity can guard a secret faithfully, it is useful because it speaks only *to those who* are worthy, that is, to the intelligent and the studious who are worthy to be admitted to the secrets of wisdom.

Then when he says: *Therefore, as customarily happens in mathematics,* etc., he shows in what order one must proceed {120}, namely, from those statements that are known through themselves; and in this regard he does two things. First, he sets down the order of proceeding; second, he indicates those statements from which he intends to proceed, where he says: *A common conception of the mind is,* etc.

He therefore states first that he intends to propose from the start certain kinds of principles, known through themselves, which he calls *terms* and *rules:* 'terms' because the resolution <back to prior principles> of all demonstrations stops at principles of this sort; 'rules,' however, because through them one is directed to a knowledge of conclusions which follow. {130} From principles of this sort he intends to draw conclusions and to make known all that ought to be developed as following logically, as happens in geometry and in other demonstrative sciences. Therefore these are called 'disciplines,' because through them 'science' is generat-

Deinde cum dicit: *Communis animi conceptio est* etc., notificat predicta principia per se nota, et primo per diffinitionem, secundo per diuisionem, ibi: *Harum autem duplex est modus* etc.

{140} Circa primum considerandum est quod huiusmodi principia, que sunt termini quia regule demonstrationum sunt, uocantur communes *animi* conceptiones. Diffinit ergo communem animi conceptionem dicens: *Communis animi conceptio est quam quisque probat auditam,* id est quam quilibet approbat statim ut eam audit. Alie enim propositiones que ex hiis demonstrantur non statim ex ipso auditu approbantur, set oportet quod per aliqua alia fiant nota. Hoc autem non est procedere {150} in infinitum, unde oportet peruenire ad aliqua que statim per se sunt nota, unde dicuntur communes animi conceptiones et communiter cadunt in conceptione cuiuslibet intellectus. Cuius ratio est quod predicatum est de ratione subiecti et ideo statim nominato subiecto et intellecto quid sit, statim manifestum est predicatum ei inesse.

Deinde cum dicit: *Harum duplex est modus,* diuidit predicta principia dicens quod predictarum communium animi conceptionum *duplex est modus.* {160} Quedam enim animi conceptiones sunt communes omnibus hominibus sicut ista: *si ab equalibus equalia auferas que relinquntur sunt equalia.* Alia *uero* est animi conceptio communis solum doctis que deriuatur a primis *animi conceptionibus* que sunt omnibus hominibus communes, et huiusmodi *est: incorporalia non esse in loco,* que *non* approbatur a uulgo *set* solum a sapientibus. Huius autem distinctionis ratio est quia cum communis animi conceptio uel principium per se notum sit aliqua {170} propositio, ex hoc quod predicatum est de ratione subiecti, si idem id quod significatur per subiectum et predicatum cadat in cognitione omnium, consequens est quod huiusmodi propositio sit per se nota omnibus, sicut quid sit equale omnibus est notum et similiter quid sit subtrahi; et ideo predicta propositio est omnibus per se nota, et

ed in the 'disciples,' thanks to the demonstration which the master propounds.

Then, when he says: *A common conception of the mind is,* etc., he indicates the aforesaid principles, known through themselves, <which will be examined> first, through definition, second, through division, where he says, *There are two sorts of these,* etc.

{140} With regard to the first one must consider that principles of this sort, which are 'terms' because they are the 'rules' of demonstrations, are called 'common conceptions *of the mind.*' Therefore he defines 'common conception of the mind' saying: *A common conception of the mind is one that everyone approves on hearing,* that is, one which anyone at all approves immediately on hearing it. For other propositions which are demonstrated from these are not approved immediately upon their very hearing, but must become known through some others. There is here, however, no progression {150} to infinity; hence it is necessary to arrive at some propositions which are known immediately through themselves. Thus these are called 'common conceptions of the mind,' and they fall commonly into the conception of any intellect whatever. The reason for this is that the predicate belongs to the intelligible structure[3] of the subject and, therefore, as soon as the subject is named and what it is is understood, the fact that the predicate is in the subject is immediately obvious.

Then when he says: *There are two sorts of these,* he divides the aforesaid principles, stating that *there are two sorts* of common conceptions of the mind. {160} For some conceptions of the mind are common to all humans, such as this one: *If from equals you subtract equals, what remain* are *equals.* The other sort, *however,* is a conception of the mind common only to the learned, and it is derived from the first *conceptions of the mind,* which are common to all humans. Of this sort *is: Incorporeal things are not in a place;* this is *not* approved by the common crowd *but* only by the wise. The reason for this distinction is as follows: A common conception of the mind, or principle known through itself, is a certain kind of {170} proposition because the predicate belongs to the intelligible structure of the subject. Thus if the same item that is signified through the subject and through the predicate falls within the understanding of all, it follows that a proposition of this sort is known through itself to all. Now

similiter: "omne totum est maius sua parte", et alia huiusmodi. Set ad apprehendendum rem incorpoream, solus intellectus sapientum consurgit, nam {180} uulgarium hominum intellectus non transcendunt ymaginationem, que est solum corporalium rerum, et ideo ea que sunt propria corporum, puta esse in loco circumscriptiue, intellectus sapientum statim remouet a rebus incorporeis, quod *uulgus* facere non potest.

what an 'equal' is is known to all, and, likewise, what 'to be subtracted' is; therefore the aforesaid proposition <If from equals you subtract equals, what remain are equals> is known through itself to all. Similar to this is "every whole is greater than its part," as well as others of this sort. But only the intellect of the wise rises to a grasp of incorporeal reality, for {180} the intellects of the common people do not transcend imagination, which bears on corporeal realities only. Therefore the properties of bodies, 'to be circumscriptively in a place,' for instance, the intellect of the wise immediately removes from incorporeal realities; this the *common crowd* cannot do.

Diuersum est esse et id quod est.

Ipsum enim esse nondum est. At uero quod est accepta essendi forma est atque consistit.

Quod est participare aliquo potest, set ipsum esse nullo modo aliquo participat. Fit enim participatio cum aliquid iam est. Est autem aliquid cum esse susceperit.

Id quod est habere aliquid preter quam quod ipsum est potest. Ipsum uero esse nichil aliud preter se habet ammixtum.

{10} Diuersum est tamen esse aliquid et esse aliquid in eo quod est.

Illic enim accidens, hic substancia significatur.

Omne quod est participat eo quod est esse ut sit. Alio uero participat ut aliquid sit.

Ac per hoc id quod est participat eo quod est esse ut sit. Est uero ut participet alio quolibet.

Omni composito aliud est esse, aliud ipsum est.

Omne simplex esse suum et id quod est unum habet.

Omnis diuersitas discors, similitudo uero appetenda {20} est.

Et quod appetit aliud, tale ipsum esse naturaliter ostenditur quale est illud hoc ipsum quod appetit.

Sufficiunt igitur que premisimus. A prudente uero rationis interprete suis unumquodque aptabitur argumentis.

EXPOSITIO

Diuersum est esse et id quod est.

Supra Boetius dixerat hoc ordine se processurum ut prius premitteret quosdam terminos et regulas ex quibus ad ulteriora procederet, et ideo secundum ordinem pretaxatum primo incipit premittere quasdam regulas siue conceptiones quasdam sapientum. Secundo ex illis incipit argumentari, ibi: *Questio uero huiusmodi est* etc.

Sicut autem dictum est, ille propositiones sunt {10} maxime note que utuntur terminis quos omnes intelligunt; ea autem que in intellectu om-

CHAPTER 2

Being and that-which-is are diverse.

For being itself as yet is not. That-which-is however, once the form of being has been taken on, is and stands together.

What-is can participate in something, but being itself in no way participates in anything. For participation occurs when something already is. Something is, however, when it has received being.

That-which-is can possess something other than what it itself is. Being itself, however, has nothing else outside itself as an admixture.

{10} *However, to be something, and to be something in this, that <a thing> is, are diverse.*

For by the former, accident is signified; by the latter, substance.

Everything that is participates in that which is being with the result that it be. It participates in something else with the result that it be something.

And through this, that-which-is participates in that which is being with the result that it be. It is, however, with the result that it can participate in anything else you like.

In every composite, being is other than the item itself.

Every simple item possesses its being and that-which-is as one.

All diversity is discordant, whereas similitude must be sought.

{20} *And what seeks something else is shown to be itself by nature such as that which it seeks.*

What we have set down as preliminaries, therefore, suffice. Each one will be applied in argumentation by the prudent interpreter of their meaning.

EXPOSITION

Being and that-which-is are diverse.

Boethius had said above that he would proceed in this order: First he would set forth certain terms and rules from which he would proceed to further points, and therefore, according to this prearranged order, he begins first to put forth certain rules or conceptions of the wise. Second, from these he begins to argue, where he says: *Now the question is of this sort*, etc. <L.3.B1>.

As was said, however, those propositions are {10} best known which use terms that all understand. Those, however, which fall within the

nium cadunt sunt maxime communia, que sunt ens, unum et bonum; et ideo primo ponit hic Boetius quasdam conceptiones pertinentes ad ens, secundo quasdam pertinentes ad unum ex quo sumitur ratio simplicis et compositi, ibi: *Omni composito* etc.; tercio ponit quasdam conceptiones pertinentes ad bonum, ibi: *Omnis diuersitas discors* etc.

Circa ens autem consideratur ipsum esse quasi {20} quiddam commune et indeterminatum, quod quidem dupliciter determinatur, uno modo ex parte subiecti quod esse habet, alio modo ex parte predicati utpote cum dicimus de homine uel de quacumque alia re, non quidem quod sit simpliciter, set quod sit aliquid puta album uel nigrum. Primo ergo ponit conceptiones que accipiuntur secundum comparationem esse ad id quod est. Secundo ponit conceptiones que accipiuntur secundum comparationem eius quod est esse {30} simpliciter ad id quod est esse aliquid, ibi: *Diuersum tamen est esse aliquid* etc.

Circa primum duo facit. Primo proponit differenciam eius quod est esse ad id quod est. Secundo manifestat huiusmodi differenciam, ibi: *Ipsum enim esse* etc.

Dicit ergo primo quod *diuersum est esse et id quod est*, que quidem diuersitas non est hic referenda ad res de quibus adhuc non loquitur, set ad ipsas rationes seu intentiones. Aliud autem significamus {40} per hoc quod dicimus esse et aliud per id quod dicimus id quod est, sicut et aliud significamus cum dicimus currere et aliud per hoc quod dicitur currens. Nam currere et esse significatur in abstracto sicut et albedo; set quod est, id est ens et currens, significatur in concreto uelud album.

Deinde cum dicit: *Ipsum enim esse* etc., manifestat predictam diuersitatem tribus modis.

Quorum primus est quia ipsum esse non significatur sicut subiectum essendi, sicut nec currere {50} significatur sicut subiectum cursus. Vnde sicut non possumus dicere quod ipsum currere currat, ita non possumus dicere quod ipsum esse sit; set id quod est significatur sicut subiectum essendi, uelud id quod currit significatur sicut subiectum currendi; et ideo sicut possumus dicere de eo quod currit siue de currente quod currat in quantum subicitur cursui et participat ipsum, ita possumus dicere

understanding of all are the most common, and these are 'being,' 'one,' and 'good.' And therefore Boethius here first sets down some conceptions pertaining to being;[4] second, some pertaining to one, from which are derived the notions of the simple and of the composite, where he says: *In every composite,* etc. Third, he lays out certain conceptions pertaining to good, where he says: *All diversity is discordant,* etc.

With regard to being, however, being itself is considered as {20} something common and indeterminate. In fact, it is determined in two ways: In one way, by the subject which possesses being; in the other way, by the predicate, as when we say of a human being or of any other reality, not that it without qualification is, but that it is something, such as white or black. First, therefore, he sets down conceptions which are derived from a comparison of being with that-which-is. Second, he lays out conceptions which are derived from a comparison of what it is to be {30} without qualification with what it is to be something, where he says: *However, to be something . . . are diverse,* etc.

Concerning the first point he does two things. First, he sets out the differentiating note of that which is being, as against that-which-is. Second, he makes this difference clear, where he says: *For being itself,* etc.

Therefore he says first that *being and that-which-is are diverse.* This diversity is not here to be referred to the realities, of which he has not yet spoken, but to the notions or intentions themselves. For we signify one thing {40} by saying 'to be,' and something else by saying 'that-which-is,' just as we also signify one thing when we say 'to run,' and something else by saying 'one running.' For 'to run' and 'to be' are signified in the abstract, just as 'whiteness' is; but 'what-is,' that is, 'a being,' and 'one running' are signified in the concrete, as is 'a white item.'

Then when he says: *For being itself,* etc., he shows the aforesaid diversity in three ways.

Of these the first is that 'to be' itself is not signified as the subject of 'being,' just as 'to run' is not {50} signified as the subject of 'running.' Hence, just as we cannot say 'to run itself runs,' so we cannot say 'to be itself is;' rather, 'that-which-is' is signified as the subject of 'being,' just as 'that which runs' is signified as the subject of 'running.' Therefore, just as we can say of that which runs or of one running that 'he runs' inasmuch as he is the subject of running and participates in it, so we can

quod ens siue id quod est sit in quantum participat actum essendi. Et hoc est quod dicit quod *ipsum* {60} *esse nondum est* quia non attribuitur sibi esse sicut subiecto essendi, set id *quod est, accepta essendi forma,* scilicet suscipiendo ipsum actum essendi, *est atque consistit,* id est in se ipso subsistit. Non enim dicitur ens proprie et per se nisi de substancia cuius est subsistere; accidencia enim non dicuntur encia quasi ipsa sint, set in quantum eis substancia est aliquid ut post dicetur.

Secundam differenciam ponit ibi: *Quod est participare* etc. Que quidem differencia sumitur {70} secundum rationem participationis. Est autem participare quasi partem capere. Et ideo quando aliquid particulariter recipit id quod ad alterum pertinet uniuersaliter, dicitur participare illud, sicut homo dicitur participare animal quia non habet rationem animalis secundum totam communitatem; et eadem ratione Sortes participat hominem. Similiter etiam subiectum participat accidens et materia formam, quia forma substancialis uel accidentalis, que de sui ratione communis est, {80} determinatur ad hoc uel illud subiectum. Et similiter etiam effectus dicitur participare suam causam, et precipue quando non adequat uirtutem sue cause, puta si dicamus quod aer participat lucem solis quia non recipit eam in claritate qua est in sole. Pretermisso autem hoc tercio modo participandi, impossibile est quod secundum duos primos modos ipsum esse participet aliquid. Non enim potest participare aliquid per modum quo materia uel subiectum participat formam uel accidens quia {90} ut dictum est ipsum esse significatur ut quiddam abstractum. Similiter autem nec potest aliquid participare per modum quo particulare participat uniuersale; sic enim etiam ea que in abstracto dicuntur participare aliquid possunt sicut albedo colorem, set ipsum esse est communissimum, unde ipsum quidem participatur in aliis, non autem participat aliquid aliud. Set id quod est siue ens, quamuis sit communissimum, tamen concretiue dicitur, et ideo participat ipsum esse, non per {100} modum quo magis commune participatur a minus communi, set participat ipsum esse per modum quo concretum participat abstractum. Hoc est ergo quod dicit quod id *quod est,* scilicet ens, *participare aliquo potest; set ipsum esse nullo modo participat aliquo;* et hoc probat ex eo quod supra dictum est, quod scilicet ipsum esse nondum est.

say that a being, or that-which-is, 'is' inasmuch as it participates in an act of being.[5] And this is what he says: That *being* {60} *itself as yet is not,* because to be is not attributed to 'to be' itself as to the subject of being, but that *which is . . . the form of being . . . taken on,* namely, by receiving the very act of being, *is and stands together,* that is, it subsists in itself. For being is not stated properly and through itself except in the case of substance, whose property it is to subsist; for accidents are not called beings as if they themselves were, but inasmuch as by them a substance is something, as will be said later.

He sets down a second difference where he says: *What-is . . . participate,* etc. This difference indeed is taken {70} in accord with the notion of participation. For 'to participate' is, as it were, 'to grasp a part.' And, therefore, when something receives in a particular way that which belongs to another in a universal way, it is said 'to participate' in that, as human being is said to participate in animal because it does not possess the intelligible structure of animal according to its total commonality; and in the same way, Socrates participates in human. And similarly, too, a subject participates in accident, and matter in form, because a substantial form, or an accidental one, which is common by virtue of its own intelligible structure, {80} is determined to this or that subject. And similarly, too, an effect is said 'to participate' in its own cause, and especially when it is not equal to the power of its cause, as for example, if we should say that 'air participates in the light of the sun' because it does not receive that light with the brilliance it has in the sun. However, setting aside this third way of participating, it is impossible that 'to be' itself participate in anything in the first two ways. For it cannot participate in anything in the way in which matter or a subject participates in a form or an accident because, {90} as has been said, 'to be' itself is signified as something abstract. Similarly, however, neither can it <'to be'> participate in anything in the way in which a particular participates in a universal. For in this way too, those things which are said in the abstract can participate in something, as 'white' can participate in color; but 'to be' itself is most common, whence indeed it is participated in by others, but still does not participate in anything else. However, that-which-is, or being, although it is most common, is nevertheless said concretely. And so it participates in 'to be' itself, not in {100} the way the more common

Manifestum est enim quod id quod non est non potest aliquo participare, unde consequens est quod *participatio* conueniat alicui *cum iam est;*
set ex hoc *aliquid est* {110} quod *suscipit* ipsum *esse* sicut dictum est. Vnde
relinquitur quod id quod est aliquid possit participare, ipsum autem esse
non possit aliquid participare.

Terciam differenciam ponit ibi: *Id quod est habere* etc. Et sumitur ista
differencia per admixtionem alicuius extranei. Circa quod considerandum est quod circa quodcumque abstracte significatum hoc habet ueritatem quod non habet in se aliquid extraneum, quod scilicet sit preter
{120} essenciam suam, sicut humanitas, albedo et quecumque hoc modo
dicuntur, cuius ratio est quia humanitas significatur ut quo aliquid est
homo, et albedo ut quo aliquid est album; non est autem aliquid homo
formaliter loquendo nisi per id quod ad rationem hominis pertinet, et
similiter non est aliquid album formaliter nisi per id quod pertinet ad rationem albi; et ideo huiusmodi abstracta nichil alienum in se habere
possunt. Aliter autem se habet in hiis que significantur in {130} concreto, nam homo significatur ut qui habet humanitatem, et album ut quod
habet albedinem. Ex hoc autem quod homo habet humanitatem uel album albedinem, non prohibetur habere aliquid aliud quod non pertinet
ad rationem horum, nisi solum quod est oppositum hiis; et ideo homo et
album possunt aliquid aliud habere quam humanitatem uel albedinem;
et hec est ratio quare albedo et humanitas significantur per modum par-
tis et non predicantur de concretis sicut nec {140} aliqua pars de suo
toto. Quia igitur, sicut dictum est, ipsum esse significatur ut abstractum,
id quod est ut concretum, consequens est uerum esse quod hic dicitur
quod id *quod est potest aliquid habere preter quam quod ipsum est,* id est
preter suam essenciam, set *ipsum esse nichil aliud habet ammixtum* preter
suam essenciam.

is participated in by the less common, but rather it participates in 'to be' itself in the way in which the concrete participates in the abstract. Therefore this is what he says, that *what-is*, namely being, *can participate in something; but being itself in no way participates in anything.*[6] And he proves this from what was stated above, namely, that 'to be' itself as yet is not. For this is evident: That-which-is-not cannot participate in anything; whence it follows that *participation* can belong to something *when it already is.* But from the fact that *it receives being* itself, {110} *something is*, as has been said. Hence this remains: That-which-is can participate in something; 'to be' itself, however, cannot participate in anything.

He sets down a third difference where he says: *That-which-is . . . possess*, etc. And this difference is grasped through the admixture of something extraneous. Concerning this, one must consider that with respect to whatever is signified abstractly, what has truth has nothing extraneous in it, namely, what is outside {120} its own essence, for instance, 'humanity,' 'whiteness,' and whatever things are said in this way. The reason for this is that 'humanity' is signified as that by which something is a human being, and 'whiteness' as that by which something is white. Now something is not human, formally speaking, except through that which pertains to the intelligible structure of a human, and similarly, nothing is formally white except through that which pertains to the intelligible structure of white. Therefore abstract things of this sort can have in themselves nothing alien. The situation is different, however, in items that are signified in {130} the concrete; for 'a human' is signified as one who possesses humanity, and 'something white,' as what possesses whiteness. However, the fact that a human possesses humanity, or a white item whiteness, does not prevent their possessing something else which does not pertain to their intelligible structures; <excluded is> only that which is opposed to them. Therefore a human and a white item can possess something other than humanity or whiteness. And this is the reason why whiteness or humanity are signified after the fashion of a part, and are not predicated of concrete items, just as {140} a part is not predicated of its whole. Therefore, as has been said, since 'to be' itself is signified as abstract, while 'that-which-is' is signified as concrete, it follows that what is stated here is true: That-*which-is can possess something other than what it itself is,* that is, something outside its own essence,

Deinde cum dicit: *Diuersum est tamen esse* etc., ponit conceptiones que accipiuntur secundum comparationem eius quod est esse simpliciter ad {150} id quod est esse aliquid. Et primo ponit utriusque diuersitatem. Secundo assignat differencias, ibi: *Illic enim accidens* etc.

Circa primum considerandum est quod ex quo id quod est potest aliquid habere preter suam essenciam, necesse est quod in eo consideretur duplex esse: quia enim forma est principium essendi, necesse est quod secundum quamlibet formam habitam habens aliqualiter esse dicatur. Si ergo forma illa non sit preter essenciam habentis, {160} set constituat eius essenciam, ex eo quod habet talem formam dicetur habens esse simpliciter, sicut homo ex hoc quod habet animam rationalem. Si uero sit talis forma que sit extranea ab essencia habentis eam, secundum illam formam non dicitur habens esse simpliciter, set esse aliquid, sicut secundum albedinem homo dicitur esse albus. Et hoc est quod dicit quod *diuersum est esse aliquid* quod non est esse simpliciter et quod *aliquid* sit *in eo quod est,* quod est proprium esse subiecti.

{170} Deinde cum dicit: *Illic enim accidens* etc., ponit tres differencias inter premissa.

Quarum prima est quod *illic,* id est ubi dicitur de re quod sit aliquid et non quod sit simpliciter, *significatur accidens,* quia forma que facit huiusmodi esse est preter essenciam rei. *Hic* autem cum dicitur aliquid esse in eo quod est, *significatur substancia,* quia scilicet forma faciens hoc esse constituit essenciam rei.

Secundam differenciam ponit ibi: *Omne quod* {180} *est* etc. Dicit quod ad hoc quod aliquid *sit* simpliciter subiectum *participat* ipsum *esse,* set ad hoc quod *sit aliquid,* oportet quod participet aliquo *alio,* sicut homo ad hoc quod sit albus participat non solum esse substanciale set etiam albedinem.

Terciam differenciam ponit ibi: *Ac per hoc* etc. Que quidem accipitur secundum ordinem utriusque et concluditur ex premissis. Est autem hec

but *being itself . . . has nothing else as an admixture* outside its own essence.

Then when he says: *However, to be . . . are diverse,* etc., he sets down conceptions which are understood by comparing what it is 'to be' without qualification with {150} what it is 'to be something.' And first he sets down the diversity of the two; second, he assigns the differences, where he says: *For by the former accident,* etc.

With regard to the first it must be considered that, since 'that-which-is' can possess something outside its essence, one must consider that there is in it a double 'to be'; for since form is a principle of being, according to any form possessed, something is said in some way to possess 'to be.' If, therefore, that form is not outside the essence of that which possesses it, {160} but constitutes that item's essence, from the fact that the item possesses such a form it will be said to have being[7] without qualification, as a human is said <to be> from the fact of possessing a rational soul. If, however, the form be such that it is extraneous to the essence of what possesses it, according to that form, the item will not be said to have being without qualification, but 'to be something,' as, thanks to whiteness, a human being is said to be white. And this is what he says: *Diverse is to be something,*[8] which is not to be without qualification, and that *something* be *in this, that it is,*[9] which is the proper being of a subject.

{170} Then when he says: *For by the former accident,* etc., he sets down three differences among the foregoing.

The first of these is that <by> *the former,* that is, where it is said of a reality that it 'is something,' and not that it without qualification 'is,' *accident is signified,* because the form which makes it to be 'of this sort' is outside the essence of the reality. <By> *the latter,* however, when something is said to be 'in this, that it is,' *substance is signified,* because the form making this reality to be constitutes its essence.

The second difference he sets down where he says: *Everything that* {180} *is,* etc. He says that for something to *be* a subject without qualification, it *participates* in *being* itself, but for it to *be something,* it must participate in something *else,* as a human, to be white, participates not only in substantial being, but in whiteness as well.

He sets down a third difference where he says: *And through this,* etc. This is understood according to the order of both <types of participa-

differencia quod primo oportet ut intelligatur {190} aliquid esse simpliciter, et postea quod sit aliquid, et hoc patet ex premissis. Nam aliquid
est simpliciter per hoc quod *participat* ipso *esse;* set quando iam *est,* scilicet
per participationem ipsius esse, restat *ut participet* quocumque *alio* ad hoc
scilicet quod sit aliquid.

Deinde cum dicit: *Omni composito* etc., ponit conceptiones de composito et simplici, que pertinent ad rationem unius, et est considerandum
quod ea que supra dicta sunt de diuersitate ipsius {200} esse et eius quod
est, est secundum ipsas intentiones. Hic ostendit quomodo applicetur ad
res; et primo ostendit hoc in compositis, secundo in simplicibus, ibi:
Omne simplex etc.

Est ergo primo considerandum quod sicut esse et quod est differunt
secundum intentiones, ita in compositis differunt realiter. Quod quidem
manifestum est ex premissis. Dictum est enim supra quod ipsum esse
neque participat aliquid ut eius ratio constituatur ex multis, neque habet {210} aliquid extrinsecum admixtum ut sit in eo compositio accidentalis; et ideo ipsum esse non est compositum; res ergo composita non est
suum esse; et ideo dicit quod in *omni composito aliud est* esse ens et *aliud*
ipsum compositum quod est participando *ipsum esse.*

Deinde cum dicit: *Omne simplex* etc., ostendit qualiter se habeat in
simplicibus in quibus necesse est quod *ipsum esse et id quod est* sit *unum* et
idem realiter. Si enim esset aliud realiter id quod est et {220} ipsum esse,
iam non esset simplex set compositum. Est tamen considerandum quod,
cum simplex dicatur aliquid ex eo quod caret compositione, nichil prohibet aliquid esse secundum quid simplex, in quantum caret aliqua
compositione, quod tamen non est omnino simplex; unde et ignis et
aqua dicuntur simplicia corpora, in quantum carent compositione que
est ex contrariis que inuenitur in mixtis, quorum tamen unumquodque
est compositum, tum ex partibus quantitatiuis, {230} tum etiam ex forma et materia. Si ergo inueniantur alique forme non in materia, unaqueque earum est quidem simplex quantum ad hoc quod caret materia,

tion> and is concluded from the prior statements. There is this difference, however: First it is necessary that something be understood {190}
to be without qualification, and afterward, that it be something, and this
is clear from the prior statements. For something is without qualification thanks to the fact that it *participates* in *being* itself. But when it already *is*, namely through participation in being itself, it remains *that it
can participate* in anything *else* with this result: that it be something.

Then when he says: *In every composite*, etc., he sets down conceptions
on the composite and the simple which pertain to the character of oneness. It must be considered that what was said above concerning the difference between {200} 'to be' itself and its 'what-is,' is in accord with
these very intentions. Here he shows how this is applied to realities; and
he shows this first in composite items, and second in simple items,
where he says: *Every simple*, etc.

Therefore it must be considered first that just as 'to be' and 'what is'
differ according to intention, so in composite items they differ in reality.
This, in fact, is manifest from the prior remarks. For it was said above
that 'to be' itself neither participates in anything, so that its character
would be constituted from many, nor does it have {210} anything ex-
trinsic admixed, so that there would be accidental composition in it.
And therefore 'to be' itself is not composite. And therefore a composite
reality is not its own 'to be,' and so he says that in *every composite it is one
thing* to be a being, and *another* to be the composite itself, which IS by
participating in *being itself*.[10]

Then when he says: *Every simple*, etc., he shows how things stand in
simple items, in which it is necessary that *being itself and that-which-is*
must be really *one* and the same. For if <an item's> that-which-is and its
{220} very 'to be' were really other, it would not be simple but composite. Still, it must be considered that, while something is said to be 'simple' because it lacks composition, nothing prevents that it be simple according to some aspect, inasmuch as it lacks a certain composition, yet
that it not be altogether simple. Hence it is that both fire and water are
said to be 'simple' bodies inasmuch as they lack the composition that results from contraries, which is found in mixed items, even though each
one of them is a composite, both of its own quantitative parts {230} and
of matter and form as well. Therefore if there should be found certain

et per consequens quantitate que est dispositio materie. Quia tamen quelibet forma est determinatiua ipsius esse, nulla earum est ipsum esse, set est habens esse; puta secundum opinionem Platonis, ponamus formam immaterialem subsistere que sit ydea et ratio hominum materialium, et aliam formam que sit ydea et {240} ratio equorum, manifestum erit quod ipsa forma immaterialis subsistens, cum sit quiddam determinatum ad speciem, non est ipsum esse commune, set participat illud. Et nichil differt quantum ad hoc si ponamus alias formas immateriales altioris gradus quam sint rationes horum sensibilium ut Aristotiles uoluit; unaqueque enim illarum, in quantum distinguitur ab alia, quedam specialis forma est participans ipsum esse, et sic nulla earum erit uere simplex. Id autem solum erit uere {250} simplex quod non participat esse, non quidem inherens set subsistens. Hoc autem non potest esse nisi unum, quia, si ipsum esse nichil aliud habet admixtum preter id quod est esse, ut dictum est, impossibile est id quod est ipsum esse multiplicari per aliquid diuersificans, et, quia nichil aliud preter se habet adiunctum, consequens est quod nullius accidentis sit susceptiuum. Hoc autem simplex, unum et sublime est ipse Deus.

Deinde cum dicit: *Omnis diuersitas* etc., ponit {260} duas conceptiones pertinentes ad appetitum ex quo diffinitur bonum, nam bonum dicitur quod omnia appetunt.

Est ergo prima conceptio quod *omnis diuersitas* est *discors* et *similitudo est appetenda*. Circa quod considerandum est quod discordia importat contrarietatem appetitus, unde illud dicitur esse discors quod repugnat appetitui; omne autem diuersum in quantum huiusmodi repugnat appetitui; cuius ratio est quia simile augetur et perficitur suo {270} simili; unumquodque autem appetit suum augmentum et perfectionem; et ideo simile in quantum huiusmodi est unicuique appetibile et pari ratione diuersum repugnat appetitui in quantum diminuit et impedit perfectionem. Et ideo dicit quod *omnis diuersitas* est *discors*, id est ab appetitu discordans; *similitudo uero est appetenda*. Contingit tamen per accidens quod aliquis appetitus abhorret simile et appetit diuersum siue contrarium, nam, sicut dictum est, unumquodque primo et per se {280} appetit

forms not in matter, each one of them is indeed simple in that it lacks matter, and as a consequence quantity, which is a disposition of matter. Nevertheless, because every <such>[11] form you like is determinative of 'to be' itself, not one of them is 'to be' itself, but rather is what possesses 'to be.' For instance, following the opinion of Plato let us suppose that an immaterial form subsists, a form that is the idea and the intelligible structure of material humans, and another form subsists that is the idea and {240} the intelligible structure of horses; it will be clear that the very immaterial subsisting form, since it is something determined to a species, is not common 'to be' itself, but participates in it. And in this regard it makes no difference whether we should posit other immaterial forms of a grade higher than would be the intelligible structures of these sensibles, as Aristotle wanted. For each of these <higher forms>, inasmuch as it is distinguished from others, is a certain special form participating in 'to be' itself, and thus not one of them would be truly simple. But that alone will be truly {250} simple which does not participate in 'to be,' not inhering, in fact, but subsisting. This, however, can be but one. For if to be itself has nothing else admixed other than that which is to be, as has been said, it is impossible that this To Be Itself be multiplied through anything diversifying It, and because It has nothing outside Itself conjoined, it follows that It is susceptible of no accident. This—Simple, One, and Sublime—is God Himself.

Then when he says: *All diversity*, etc., he sets down {260} two conceptions pertaining to appetite from which 'the good' is defined, for the good is said to be 'what all things seek.'

Therefore the first conception is: *All diversity* is *discordant* and *similitude must be sought*. With regard to this it must be considered that discord implies a contrariety of appetite; wherefore that is said to be discordant which is repugnant to appetite. However, everything diverse, inasmuch as it is of this sort, is repugnant to an appetite. The reason for this is as follows: Like is increased and brought to completion by its own {270} like. Now everything seeks its own increase and completion, and on this account what is like, inasmuch as it is such, is for each reality that which is sought. And for a parallel reason the diverse is repugnant to an appetite inasmuch as it diminishes and impedes completion. Therefore he says that *All diversity* is *discordant*, that is, discordant with respect to appetite, *whereas similitude must be sought*. It happens by accident, however,

suam perfectionem que est bonum uniuscuiusque et est semper propor-
tionata perfectibili, et secundum hoc habet similitudinem ad ipsum. Alia
uero que sunt exterius appetuntur uel refutantur in quantum conferunt
ad propriam perfectionem, a qua quidem deficit quandoque aliquid per
defectum, quandoque autem per excessum, nam propria perfectio
uniuscuiusque rei in quadam commensuratione consistit, sicut perfectio
corporis humani consistit in commensurato calore, a {290} quo si deficiat appetit aliquod calidum per quod calor augeatur; si autem superexce-
dat, appetit contrarium, scilicet frigidum, per quod ad temperamentum
reducatur, in quo consistit perfectio conformis nature. Et sic etiam unus
figulus abhorret alium, in quantum scilicet aufert ei perfectionem
desideratam, scilicet lucrum.

Secundam autem conceptionem ponit ibi: *Et quod appetit* etc., que
concluditur ex premissa. Si enim similitudo per se est appetenda, consequenter {300} id *quod appetit aliud ostenditur tale naturaliter esse quale est hoc
quod appetit,* quia scilicet naturalem inclinationem habet ad id quod appetit; que quidem naturalis inclinatio quandoque sequitur ipsam essenciam rei, sicut graue appetit esse deorsum secundum rationem sue
essencialis nature; quandoque uero consequitur naturam alicuius forme
superuenientis, sicut cum aliquis habet habitum acquisitum desiderat id
quod conuenit ei secundum habitum illum.

{310} Vltimo autem epilogat et dicit quod *sufficiunt* ad propositum ea
que premissa sunt et quod ille qui prudenter interpretatur rationes dicto-
rum poterit *unumquodque* eorum adaptare congruis *argumentis,* applican-
do scilicet ea ad debitas conclusiones ut patebit in sequentibus.

that a certain appetite may abhor the similar and seek the diverse or the contrary. For, as has been said, everything primarily and of itself {280} seeks its own completion, which is 'the good' of each one and is always proportioned to what can be completed, and in this regard has a similitude with respect to it <the thing completed>. Other things, however, are sought or refused in a more external way inasmuch as they contribute to its own completion from which, in fact, at times something falls away, sometimes through defect, but sometimes through excess. For the appropriate completion of each thing consists in a certain measure, as the completion of a human body consists in a measure of heat; {290} if this should be deficient it <the human body> seeks something hot through which the heat might be increased. If, however, it should go beyond that measure, it seeks the contrary, namely, something cold through which it might be led back to the temperate grade in which a completion in conformity with nature consists. And thus, too, one potter abhors another inasmuch as he takes away his desired completion, namely gain.

Now he sets down a second conception where he says: *And what seeks*, etc., which is concluded from the previous remarks. For if similitude of itself must be sought, it follows that {300} *what seeks something else is shown to be itself by nature such as that which it seeks,* because, namely, it has a natural inclination toward that which it seeks. That natural inclination sometimes follows the very essence of a reality, as the heavy seeks to be below, in accord with the intelligible structure of its essential nature. Sometimes, however, it follows the nature of some supervenient form; for instance, when someone possesses an acquired habit he desires that which suits him in accord with that habit.

{310} Finally he writes an epilogue and says that for his purpose *what* <were set down as> preliminaries *suffice,* and that one who interprets prudently the meanings of the things that have been said will be able to adapt *each one* of them to suitable *argumentation,* namely, by applying them to due conclusions, as will be evident in what follows.

Questio uero huiusmodi est: ea que sunt bona sunt; tenet enim communis sentencia doctorum omne quod est ad bonum tendere, omne autem tendit ad simile; que igitur ad bonum tendunt bona ipsa sunt.

Set quemadmodum bona sint inquirendum est utrumne participatione an substancia.

Si participatione, per se ipsa nullo modo bona sunt; nam quod participatione album est, per se in eo quod ipsum est album non est; et de ceteris qualitatibus {10} eodem modo. Si igitur participatione sunt bona, ipsa per se nullo modo bona sunt; non igitur ad bonum tendunt; set concessum est. Non igitur participatione sunt bona set substancia.

Quorum uero substancia bona est id quod sunt bona sunt. Id quod sunt autem habent ex eo quod est esse. Esse igitur ipsorum bonum est. Omnium igitur rerum ipsum esse bonum est. Set si esse bonum est ea que sunt in eo quod sunt bona sunt. Idemque illis est esse quod bonis esse. Substancialia igitur bona sunt quoniam non {20} participant bonitatem. Quod si ipsum esse in eis bonum est, non est dubium quin, substancialia cum sint bona, primo sint bono similia. Ac per hoc, ipsum bonum erunt. Nichil enim illi preter se ipsum simile est. Ex quo fit ut omnia que sunt Deus sint, quod dictu nephas est. Non sunt igitur substancialia bona. Ac per hoc non in hiis est esse bonum. Non sunt igitur in eo quod sunt bona.

Set nec participant bonitatem. Nullo enim modo ad bonum tenderent. Nullo modo igitur sunt bona.

EXPOSITIO

Questio uero huiusmodi est.

Premissis quibusdam principiis que sunt necessaria ad proposite questionis discussionem, hic accedit ad questionem propositam, et circa hoc tria facit. Primo proponit questionem. Secundo adhibet solutionem, ibi: *Huic questioni talis poterit* etc. Tercio excludit quasdam conclusiones contra solutionem, ibi: *At non etiam alba* etc.

CHAPTER 3

Now the question is of this sort: Those things that are, are good; for the common opinion of the learned holds that everything that is tends to the good; everything, however, tends to its like; therefore, things that tend to the good are themselves good.

But one must inquire as to the way in which they might be good: whether by participation or by substance.

If by participation, they are in no manner good through themselves; for what is white by participation is not white through itself, that is, insofar as it itself is. The same holds concerning {10} other qualities. If, therefore, they <things that are> are good by participation, through themselves they are in no way good. Therefore, they do not tend to the good. But that <they do> has been conceded. Therefore, they are good not by participation, but by substance.

Of those things, however, whose substance is good, that which they are is[12] good. That which they are, however, they possess from that which is being. Therefore their being is good; therefore, the very being[13] of all things is good. But if <their> being is good, those things that are, are good insofar as they are, and for them to be is the same as to be good. Therefore they are substantial goods because they do not {20} participate in goodness. But if in them being itself is good, there is no doubt that, since they are substantial goods, they are similar to the First Good. And because of this, they will be the Good Itself, for there is nothing outside Itself which is like It. From this it results that all things that are would be God, which it is wicked to say. Therefore they are not substantial goods and, owing to this, in them being is not good. Therefore, they are not good in this, that they are.

But neither do they participate in goodness, for then in no way would they tend to the good. In no way, therefore, are they good.

EXPOSITION

Now the question is of this sort.

Having set down beforehand certain principles which are necessary for the discussion of the question proposed, he here approaches that question, and in this regard he does three things. First, he puts forth the question. Second, he adds a solution, where he says: *To the question this sort . . . could,* etc. <L.4.B1>. Third, he excludes certain conclusions

Circa primum duo facit. Primo premittit quid {10} questio presup-
ponat. Secundo quid in questione dubium uersetur, ibi: *Quemadmodum
bona sunt* etc.

Dicit ergo primo sic esse ad questionem propositam accedendum ut
presupponamus quod omnia ea que sunt, bona sunt. Et ad hoc proban-
dum inducit rationem secundum premissa, que talis est: unumquodque
tendit ad suum simile, unde, ut supra premissum est, quod appetit aliud
tale ipsum esse naturaliter ostenditur quale est hoc ipsum quod appetit.
Set *omne quod est ad bonum* {20} *tendit;* et hoc quidem inducit secundum
communem *doctorum* sentenciam, unde et in I Ethicorum Philosophus
dicit quod "bonum enunciauerunt" sapientes esse "id quod omnia appetunt". Est enim proprium obiectum appetitus bonum sicut sonus proprium obiectum auditus. Vnde sicut sonus est qui percipitur ab omni auditu, ita oportet bonum esse in quod tendit omnis appetitus. Et ita cum
cuiuslibet rei sit aliquis appetitus uel intellectiuus uel sensitiuus uel naturalis, consequens est {30} quod quelibet res appetat bonum; et ita concluditur quod omnis res sit bona, quod questio intenta supponit.

Deinde cum dicit: *Set quemadmodum bona* etc., ostendit quid dubium
in questione uersetur. Et circa hoc tria facit. Primo proponit questionem.
Secundo obicit contra utrumque membrum questionis, ibi: *Si participatione* etc. Tercio ex hoc ulterius procedit ad excludendum primam suppositionem, ibi: *Non sunt ergo in eo quod sunt bona* etc.

{40} Dicit ergo primo quod supposito omnia esse bona *inquirendum est*
de modo, quomodo scilicet bona sunt. Dupliciter autem aliquid de
aliquo dicitur, uno modo substancialiter, alio modo per participationem.
Est ergo questio utrum encia sint bona per essenciam uel per participationem. Ad intellectum autem huius questionis considerandum est quod
in ista questione supponitur quod aliquid esse per essenciam et per participationem sunt opposita. Et in uno quidem {50} supradictorum participationis modorum manifeste hoc uerum est, scilicet secundum illum

against the solution, where he says: *But . . . not also . . . white things,* etc.
<L.5.B23>.

With regard to the first point he does two things. First, he lays out in
advance what {10} the question presupposes, and second, what doubt is
involved in the question, where he says: *The way in which they are good,*
etc.

Therefore he says first that the question proposed must be ap-
proached thus: that we presuppose that all the things that are, are good.
And to prove this he introduces an argument in accord with the preliminaries, which is this: Everything *tends to its own like;* whence, as was set
down above, what seeks something else is shown to be by nature such
as that which it seeks. But *everything that is tends to* {20} *the good;* and this
point he introduces in accord with the common opinion *of the learned;*
whence in I 'Ethics' The Philosopher says that the wise "have declared
the good" to be "that which all things seek."[14] For the proper object of
appetite is the good, just as sound is the proper object of hearing. Hence,
just as sound is what is perceived in every instance of hearing, so the
good must be that to which every appetite tends. Now since there is
some appetite in every thing, whether intellective or sensitive or natural, it follows {30} that every thing you like seeks a good; and thus it is
concluded that every thing is good, which the question intended sup-
poses.

Then when he says: *But . . . the way . . . good,* etc., he shows what
doubt is involved in the question. And with regard to this, he does three
things. First, he poses the question. Second, he objects against both
members of the question, where he says: *If by participation,* etc. Third,
from this he proceeds further to exclude the first supposition, where he
says: *Therefore, they are not good in this, that they are,* etc.

{40} First he says, therefore, that supposing all things are good, *one
must inquire* as to the manner, namely, how they are good. For something is said of anything in two ways: in one way, substantially, in the
other way, through participation. Therefore, the question is whether beings are good through essence, or through participation. An understanding of this question requires a consideration of its presupposition
that for something 'to be through essence' and 'to be through participation' are opposites. And in one of {50} the above-mentioned modes of

modum quo subiectum dicitur participare accidens uel materia formam. Est enim accidens preter substanciam subiecti et forma preter ipsam substanciam materie. Set in alio participationis modo, quo scilicet species participat genus, hoc etiam uerum est secundum sentenciam Platonis qui posuit aliam esse ydeam animalis et bipedis et hominis; set secundum Aristotilis sentenciam qui posuit quod {60} homo uere est id quod est animal, quasi essencia animalis non existente preter differenciam hominis, nichil prohibet id quod per participationem dicitur etiam substancialiter predicari. Boetius autem hic loquitur secundum illum participationis modum quo subiectum participat accidens, et ideo ex opposito diuidit id quod substancialiter et participatiue predicatur, ut patet per exempla que subsequenter inducit.

Deinde cum dicit: *Si participatione* etc., obicit {70} contra utrumque membrum questionis, et primo contra hoc quod res sint bone per participationem, secundo contra hoc quod sint bone secundum suam substanciam, ibi: *Quorum uero substancia* etc.

Dicit ergo primo quod si omnia sunt bona per participationem, sequitur quod *nullo modo* sint *bona per se;* et hoc quidem uerum est si per se accipiatur inesse quod ponitur in diffinitione eius de quo dicitur, sicut homo per se est animal. Quod enim ponitur in diffinitione alicuius pertinet ad essenciam {80} eius, et ita non dicitur de eo per participationem de qua nunc loquimur. Si uero accipiatur per se secundum alium modum, prout scilicet subiectum ponitur in diffinitione predicati, sic esset falsum quod hic dicitur, nam proprium accidens secundum hunc modum per se inest subiecto, et tamen participatiue de eo predicatur. Sic igitur Boetius hic accipit participationem prout subiectum participat accidens, per se autem quod ponitur in diffinitione subiecti; et sic ex necessitate {90} sequitur quod si res sint bone per participationem non sint bone per se, et hoc manifestat per exemplum; *nam* illud *quod est album* per participationem *non est album per se,* id est *in eo quod est ipsum* quod pertinet ad primum modum dicendi per se; et simile est de aliis *qualitatibus.* Sic igitur *si* encia *sunt bona* per participationem, sequitur

participation this is manifestly true, namely, according to that mode by which a subject is said to participate in an accident, or matter in a form. For an accident is outside the substance of a subject, and form is outside the very substance of matter. But in the other mode of participation, namely that by which species participates in genus, this <opposition> is also true according to the opinion of Plato, who held that the idea of 'animal' is other than 'biped' and 'human.' But according to the opinion of Aristotle, who held that {60} a human is truly that which is animal—the essence of 'animal,' as it were, not existing outside the differentiating notes of 'human'—nothing prohibits that what is said through participation also be predicated substantially.[15] Here, however, Boethius speaks according to that mode of participation by which a subject participates in an accident, and therefore he divides as opposites that which is predicated substantially and that predicated by participation, as is clear through the examples which he subsequently introduces.

Then when he says: *If by participation*, etc., he objects {70} against both members of the question: First against this, that things might be good through participation; second, against this, that they might be good according to their own substance, where he says: *Of those things, however, whose substance*, etc.

Therefore he says first that if all things are good through participation, it follows that *in no manner* would they be *good through themselves.* And this indeed is true if 'through themselves' be taken for the inherence that is posited in the definition of what is defined,[16] as a human being 'through itself' is an animal. For what is posited in the definition of anything pertains to its {80} essence, and thus is not predicated of it through the participation of which we are now speaking. If, however, 'through itself' be taken according to the other mode, namely, for the way a subject is posited in the definition of a predicate, it would be false to say this <that what is good through participation cannot be good through itself>. For a proper accident is in a subject according to this mode of 'through itself' and yet is predicated of it <the subject> by way of participation. Boethius, therefore, here takes 'participation' for the way in which a subject participates in an accident, but he takes 'through itself' for the way in which something is posited in the definition of a subject. And so it necessarily {90} follows that if things were good

quod non sint *bona per se,* id est per suam substanciam. Ex hoc ergo sequitur quod substancie encium *non* tendant ad bona, cuius contrarium
superius est {100} concessum, scilicet quod omnia in bonum tendant.
Videtur ergo quod encia non sint bona per participationem *set* per suam
substanciam.

Deinde cum dicit: *Quorum uero substancia* etc., obicit in contrarium in
hunc modum: illa *quorum substancia bona est,* necesse est quod bona sint
secundum *id* ipsum *quod sunt.* Hoc enim ad substanciam cuiusque rei
pertinet quod concurrit ad suum esse, set quod aliqua sint, hoc *habent ex
eo quod est esse:* dictum est enim supra quod est aliquid {110} cum esse
susceperit. Sequitur igitur ut eorum que sunt bona secundum substanciam ipsum *esse* sit *bonum;* si igitur omnia sunt bona secundum suam substanciam, sequetur quod omnium rerum ipsum esse sit bonum, et, quia
premissa ex quibus in argumentando processit sunt conuertibilia, procedit e conuerso. Sequitur enim e conuerso *quod si esse* omnium rerum
sit *bonum* quod ea que sunt, in quantum sunt, bona sunt, ita scilicet
quod idem sit unicuique rei *esse* et bonum *esse.* Sequitur {120} igitur
quod sint substancialia bona ex hoc quod sunt bona, et tamen non per
participationem bonitatis. Ex hoc autem quid inconueniens sequatur ostendit subdens, et dicit quod si ipsum esse rerum omnium sit bonum,
cum ex hoc sequatur quod *sint substancialia bona,* consequens est quod
sint etiam *primo bono similia* quod est substanciale bonum et cui idem est
esse et bonum esse. Et ex hoc ulterius sequitur quod omnia sint *ipsum
primum bonum,* quia *nichil preter se ipsum* est *simile* {130} *illi,* scilicet
quantum ad modum bonitatis; nichil autem aliud preter primum bonum eodem modo est bonum sicut ipsum, quia ipsum solum est primum
bonum. Dicuntur tamen aliqua ei similia in quantum sunt secundario
bona deriuata ab ipso primo et principali bono. Si ergo omnia sunt ipsum primum bonum, cum ipsum primum bonum nichil sit aliud quam
Deus, sequitur quod omnia encia *sint Deus, quod* etiam dicere *nephas est.*
Sequitur igitur et ea que premissa sunt esse falsa. *Non* {140} *igitur* encia

through 'participation,' they would not be good 'through themselves,' and this he shows through an example. *For what is white* through participation *is not white through itself*, that is, *in that which it is itself*,[17] which belongs to the first mode of saying 'through itself'; and it is similar for other *qualities*. Therefore, *if* beings *are good* through participation, it follows that they are not *good through themselves*, that is, through their own substance. From this it follows, therefore, that the substances of beings do *not* tend to goods, the contrary of which has been {100} conceded above—namely, that all things do tend to good. It seems, therefore, that beings are good not through participation, *but* through their substance.

Then when he says: *However, whose substance*, etc., he objects in a contrary way: As to those things *whose substance is good*, it is necessary that they be good according to *that* itself *which they are*. For this pertains to the substance of each thing: that it concurs with its own 'being.' But that certain things might 'be,' this *they possess from that which is being*, for it was said above that something is {110} when it has received 'to be.'[18] It follows, therefore, that of those things that are good according to substance, *being* itself is *good*. If, therefore, all things are good according to their substance, it will follow that the very 'being' of all things is good. And since the premisses from which he has proceeded in his argument are convertibles, he reasons from their converse. For it follows from the converse *that if the being* of all things be *good*, then those things that are, inasmuch as they are, are good, namely, in such a way that '*to be*' and '*to be* good' are the same for each thing. Therefore {120} it follows that they are substantial goods from this: that they are good and yet not through participation in goodness. However, he shows from this that something unsuitable would follow: He says that if the 'being' itself of all things were good, since this would entail that *they are substantial goods*, the result is that *they are* as well *similar to the First Good*, which is the Substantial Good and He for Whom 'To Be' and 'To Be Good' are the same. And from this it follows further that all things must be the First *Good Itself*, because *nothing outside Itself* is *like* {130} *It*, namely, with regard to the measure of goodness. Now nothing else outside the First Good is good in the same way as It, because It alone is the First Good. Nevertheless, some things are said to be like It inasmuch as they are goods in a secondary way, derived from that First and Principal Good

sunt substancialia bona, neque *in* eis ipsum *esse est bonum,* quia ex hiis con-
clusum est quod omnia sint Deus, et ulterius sequitur quod *non* omnia
sunt bona in quantum sunt.

Deinde cum dicit: *Set nec participant* etc., procedit ulterius ad re-
mouendum primam suppositionem et dicit quod si huic quod est encia
non esse substancialiter bona adiungatur alia conclusio que supra induc-
ta est, scilicet quod encia non sint participatiue bona quia per hoc sequeretur quod {150} *nullo modo ipsa ad bonum tenderent* ut supra habitum
est, uidetur ulterius posse concludi quod *nullo modo* encia sint *bona,*
quod est contra id quod supra premissum est.

Itself. Therefore if all things are the First Good Itself, since the First Good Itself is nothing other than God, it follows that all beings *would be God, which* even to say *is wicked*. It follows too, therefore, that those things which were set down before are false. *Therefore,* {140} beings *are not substantial goods,* nor is it that case that *in* them their very *being is good,* since from these points it was concluded that all things must be God. And it follows further that *not* all things *are good* inasmuch as they are.

Then when he says: *But neither do they participate,* etc., he proceeds further to removing the first supposition. And he says that if to this claim, which is that beings are not substantially good, there be added the other conclusion which was introduced above, namely that beings are not good by participation—for from this it would follow that {150} *in no way would they tend to the good,* as was held above—it seems that it can be further concluded that *in no way* would beings be *good,* which is opposed to what was set down above.

Huic questioni talis poterit adhibere solutio. Multa sunt que cum separari actu non possunt, animo tamen et cogitatione separantur. Vt cum triangulum uel cetera a subiecta materia nullus actu separat, mente tamen segregans ipsum triangulum proprietatemque eius preter materiam speculatur.

Amoueamus igitur primi boni presenciam paulisper ex animo, quod esse quidem constat idque ex omnium doctorum indoctorumque sentencia barbararumque {10} gentium religionibus cognosci potest.

Hoc igitur paulisper amoto, ponamus omnia esse que sunt bona atque ea consideremus quemadmodum bona esse possent si a primo bono minime defluxissent. Hinc intueor aliud in eis esse quod bona sunt, aliud quod sunt. Ponatur enim una eademque substancia bona esse, alba, grauis, rotunda. Tunc aliud esset ipsa illa substancia, aliud eius rotunditas, aliud color, aliud bonitas. Nam si hec singula idem essent quod ipsa substancia, idem esset grauitas quod color, quod {20} bonum, et bonum quod grauitas; quod fieri natura non sinit. Aliud igitur tunc in eis esset esse, aliud aliquid esse; ac tunc bona quidem essent, esse tamen ipsum minime haberent bonum. Igitur si ullo modo essent, non a bono ac bona essent; ac non idem essent quod bona, set eis aliud esset esse, aliud bonis esse.

Quod si nichil aliud essent nisi bona neque grauia neque colorata neque spacii dimensione distenta nec ulla in eis qualitas esset nisi tantum bona essent, tunc non res, set rerum uiderentur esse principium; {30} nec potius uiderentur set uideretur. Vnum enim solumque est huiusmodi quod tantum bonum aliudque nichil sit.

Que quoniam non sunt simplicia nec esse omnino poterant nisi ea id quod solum bonum est esse uoluisset. Idcirco quoniam esse eorum a boni uoluntate defluxit bona esse dicuntur. Primum enim bonum quoniam est in eo quod est bonum est. Secundum uero bonum quoniam ex eo fluxit cuius ipsum esse bonum est ipsum quoque bonum est. Set ipsum esse omnium rerum ex {40} eo fluxit quod est primum bonum et quod bonum tale est ut recte dicatur in eo quod est

To the question this sort of solution could apply: There are many things, which, although they cannot be separated in actuality, nevertheless are separated by mind and in thought. Thus no one actually separates a triangle or other such items from the underlying matter; nevertheless, distinguishing it in the mind one contemplates the triangle itself and its property outside matter.

Let us remove from the mind, therefore, the presence of the First Good for a little while, although it is obvious that It is, which can be known from the conviction of all the learned and of the unlearned, as well as from the {10} religions of the barbarous nations.

This, therefore, removed for a little while, let us suppose that all things that are are good, and let us consider how they could be good if they should in no way have flowed down from the First Good. Here I observe that in them that 'they are good' is other than that 'they are.' For let it be supposed that one and the same substance is good, white, heavy, round. Then that very substance would be one thing, its rotundity another, its color another, its goodness another. For if each of these were the same as its very substance, then weight would be the same as color, <color> the same as {20} good, and good the same as weight, which nature does not permit to happen. Therefore, in them it must be one thing to be, another to be something; and then indeed they might be good, but, nevertheless, they would not possess <their> being itself as good. Therefore, if they were <i.e., had being> in any way, and were not from the Good, and yet they were good, <the fact> that they were, would not be the same as <the fact> that they were good; rather, for them to-be would be other than to-be-good.

But if they were nothing else at all except good, neither heavy nor colored nor distended by spatial dimension, nor were there any quality in them except only that they were good, then they would seem not to be things, but the Principle of things; {30} nor would they seem, but rather It would seem. For One alone is of this sort—That It be only Good and nothing else.

Because they are not simple, they could not be at all unless That Which alone is Good had willed them to be. Therefore, since their being has flowed down from the will of the Good, they are said to be good. For the First Good, because It is, is Good in this, that It is. The second good, however, because it has flowed from It Whose Being Itself is Good, is itself also good. But the very being of all things {40} has flowed from That Which is the First Good and which is such a Good that it

esse bonum. Ipsum igitur eorum esse bonum est. Tunc enim in eo quod essent non essent bona si a primo bono minime defluxissent.

EXPOSITIO

Huic questioni talis poterit etc.

Premissa questione et rationibus hic inde inductis, hic Boetius adhibet solutionem, et circa hoc tria facit. Primo determinat ueritatem questionis. Secundo soluit obiectionem, ibi: *Qua in re soluta est questio*. Tercio inducit quasdam obiectiones circa solutionem et soluit eas, ibi: *At non etiam alba* etc.

Circa primum tria facit. Primo premittit quandam {10} suppositionem. Secundo ostendit quid illa suppositione facta sequatur circa bonitatem rerum, ibi: *Hoc igitur paulisper* etc. Tercio ostendit qualiter se habeat bonitas rerum secundum rei ueritatem nulla falsa suppositione facta, ibi: *Que quoniam non sunt simplicia* etc.

Circa primum duo facit. Primo premittit quiddam quod est necessarium ad ostendendum quod possit fieri talis suppositio. Secundo suppositionem inducit, ibi: *Amoueamus igitur* etc.

{20} Dicit ergo primo quod *multa sunt que non possunt actu separari,* que *tamen animo et cogitatione separantur,* cuius ratio est quia alio modo sunt res in anima et alio modo sunt in materia. Potest ergo esse quod aliquid ex ipso modo quo est in materia habeat inseparabilem coniunctionem ad aliud, et tamen secundum quod est in anima non habeat inseparabilem coniunctionem ad ipsum, quia scilicet ratio unius est distincta a ratione alterius; et ponit exemplum de triangulo et aliis mathematicis que {30} a materia sensibili actu separari non possunt, cum tamen mathematicus abstrahendo *mente* consideret *triangulum* et proprietatem *eius preter materiam* sensibilem, quia scilicet ratio trianguli non dependet a materia sensibili.

can rightly be said to be Good in this, that It is. Therefore, their very being is good. For if they <secondary goods> had not flowed down from the First Good, then they would not be good insofar as they are.

EXPOSITION

To the question this sort . . . could etc.

Having first set down the question and then introduced the arguments, Boethius here provides the solution, and concerning this he does three things. First, he determines the truth of the question. Second, he solves an objection, where he says: *In this very point the question has been solved* <L.5.B1>. Third, he introduces certain objections with regard to the solution and solves them, where he says: *But . . . not also . . . white things*, etc. <L.5.B23>.

With respect to the first point he does three things. First, he puts forth a certain preliminary {10} supposition. Second, he shows what would follow with regard to the goodness of things should that supposition be made, where he says: *This, therefore . . . for a little while*, etc. Third, he shows how according to the truth of the matter, no false supposition having been made, the goodness of things stands, where he says: *Because they are not simple*, etc.

With regard to the first he does two things. First, he lays out in advance something needed to show that such a supposition can be made. Second, he introduces the supposition, where he says: *Let us remove . . . therefore*, etc.

{20} He says first, therefore, that *many things which, although they cannot be separated in actuality* <are those> which *nevertheless are separated by mind and in thought*. The reason for this is that things are in the soul in one way, but they are in matter in another way. Therefore, something can possess an inseparable conjunction with something else because of the very way it is in matter and, nevertheless, according as it is in a soul, not have such an inseparable conjunction, because the intelligible structure of the one thing is distinct from that of the other. And he offers the example of a triangle and other mathematicals which {30} cannot be separated actually from sensible matter. Yet a mathematician, by abstracting *in* his *mind,* might consider *triangle* and *its* property *outside matter,* which is sensible. For the intelligible structure of a triangle does not depend upon sensible matter.

Deinde cum dicit: *Amoueamus igitur* etc., ponit suppositionem quam intendit, ut scilicet secundum considerationem mentis remoueamus ad tempus *presenciam primi boni* a ceteris rebus, quod quidem possibile est secundum ordinem cognoscibilium {40} quo ad nos. Quamuis enim secundum naturalem ordinem cognoscendi Deus sit primum cognitum, tamen quo ad nos prius sunt cogniti effectus sensibiles eius; et ideo nichil prohibet in consideratione nostra cadere effectus summi boni absque hoc quod ipsum primum bonum consideremus, ita tamen quod primum bonum non remoueamus a consideratione mentis, *quod* omnino constet nobis illud *esse*. Hoc enim *cognosci potest ex* communi omnium *sentencia* tam *doctorum* quam *indoctorum*, {50} et ulterius etiam ex ipsis *religionibus gencium barbararum* que nulle essent si Deus non est.

Deinde cum dicit: *Hoc igitur paulisper amoto* etc., ostendit quid hac suppositione facta sequatur circa bonitatem rerum, et circa hoc duo facit. Primo manifestat quod intendit. Secundo probat quiddam quod supposuerat, ibi: *Quod si nichil aliud* etc.

Dicit ergo primo quod remoto per intellectum primo bono, *ponamus* quod cetera que sunt sint {60} *bona,* quia ex bonitate effectuum deuenimus in cognitionem primi boni. *Consideremus* ergo qualiter *possent esse bona si* non processissent *a primo bono*. Hac enim suppositione facta, uidetur *in eis aliud esse* ipsa bonitas et ipsum eorum esse. Si enim *ponatur una* et *eadem substancia esse bona, alba, grauis, rotunda,* sequetur quod *aliud* in *illa* re *esset* eius *substancia, aliud rotunditas, aliud color, aliud bonitas.* Intelligitur enim bonitas uniuscuiusque rei uirtus ipsius per quam perficit operationem bonam, nam {70} uirtus est que bonum facit habentem et opus eius bonum reddit, ut patet per Philosophum in libro Ethicorum. Quod autem ista sunt aliud quam substancia rei, probat per hoc quod *singula* premissorum, *si essent idem quod* rei substancia, sequeretur quod etiam omnia illa essent eadem ad inuicem, scilicet quod *idem esset grauitas quod color* et quod bonum et quod album et quod rotunditas, quia que uni et eidem sunt eadem sibi inuicem sunt eadem; hoc autem *natura* rerum *non* patitur quod {80} omnia ista sint idem. Relinquitur *igi-*

Then when he says: *Let us remove . . . therefore*, etc., he sets down the supposition which he intends, namely, that with respect to the mind's consideration we remove temporarily *the presence of the First Good* from other things. This indeed is possible in accord with the order of things as knowable {40} to us. For although God is the First Known according to the natural order of knowing, nevertheless with regard to us His sensible effects are prior known. Therefore nothing prevents the effects of the Highest Good from falling under our consideration, without our adverting to the First Good Itself, in such a way that nevertheless we not remove the First Good from our mind's consideration, since it is altogether obvious to us *that* It *is*. For this *can be known from* the common *conviction* both *of . . . the learned* and *of the unlearned,* {50} and even beyond, from the very *religions of barbarous nations*—none of which would be the case if there were no God.

Then when he says: *This, therefore, removed for a little while,* etc., he shows, given this supposition, what would follow with regard to the goodness of things, and concerning this he does two things. First, he shows what he intends <to do>. Second, he proves something which he had presupposed, where he says: *But if they were nothing else at all except,* etc.

Therefore, he says first that, having removed by intellect the First Good, *let us suppose* that other things which are {60} *good,* since we come to a knowledge of the First Good from the goodness of Its effects. *Let us consider,* therefore, how *they could be good if* they did not proceed *from the First Good.* This supposition <that they did not proceed from the First Good> having been made, it is seen that *in them* their very goodness *is other* than their very being. For if *it be supposed that one* and *the same substance is good, white, heavy, round,* this would follow: In *that* reality its *substance would be one thing, its rotundity another, its color another, its goodness another.* For the goodness of each thing is understood to be the virtue through which it completes a good operation. For {70} virtue is what makes its possessor good and renders its work good, as is evident through The Philosopher in the book of the 'Ethics.'[19] That these <properties> are something other than the substance of the thing he proves through this: It would follow that *each* of the aforesaid, *if . . . these were the same as* the substance of the thing, would also all be identical with

tur quod premissa suppositione facta *aliud esset* in rebus ipsum *esse* et *aliud aliquid esse,* puta uel bonum uel album uel quicquid taliter dicitur, et sic predicta positione facta omnes res *essent* quidem bone, non tamen *ipsum* eorum esse esset *bonum.* Sic ergo *si* aliquo *modo essent non* a primo bono et tamen in se essent *bona,* sequeretur quod *non idem* esset in eis quod sint talia et *quod* sint *bona, set aliud esset* in *eis esse et aliud* bonum *esse.*

{90} Deinde cum dicit: *Quod si nichil aliud* etc., probat quod suppo-suerat, scilicet quod predicta suppositione facta aliud esset in eis bonum esse et aliud simpliciter esse uel quicquid aliud esse, quia si *nichil aliud* esset in eis *nisi* quod sunt *bona,* ita scilicet quod *neque* essent *grauia neque colorata neque distincta* aliqua *spacii dimensione,* sicut sunt omnia corpora, *non esset in eis ulla qualitas nisi* hoc solum quod *bona essent; tunc non* uideretur quod essent *res* create, set quod essent ipsum primum *rerum* {100} *principium,* quia id quod est ipsa essencia bonitatis est primum re-rum principium, et per consequens sequeretur quod non oporteret dicere pluraliter de omnibus eis quod *uiderentur* esse rerum principium, *set* singulariter quod *uideretur* esse primum rerum principium, tanquam omnes res bone essent simpliciter unum, quia *solum unum est* quod est *huiusmodi* ut sit *tantummodo bonum* et *nichil aliud.* Hoc autem patet esse falsum, ergo et primum, quod scilicet res create, amoto primo bono, nichil aliud {110} essent quam hoc quod est esse bonum.

Deinde cum dicit: *Que quoniam non sunt* etc., ostendit quid sit iudican-dum de bonitate rerum secundum ueritatem, et dicit quod quia res cre-ate non habent omnimodam simplicitatem, ut scilicet nichil aliud sit in eis quam essencia bonitatis, *nec* etiam *omnino esse* possent in rerum natu-ra *nisi uoluisset ea esse* Deus qui est *id quod solum bonum est,* in quantum

each other; namely, *weight would be the same as color,* and as good, and as white, and as rotundity, because things which are identical with one and the same are identical with each other. However, the *nature* of things does *not* tolerate that {80} all these be the same. *Therefore,* given the supposition noted above, it remains that in realities *it must be one thing to be* and *another to be something,* for instance, good or white or whatever else might be said in such a way. Thus the aforesaid position having been granted, all things indeed *might be* good; nevertheless, their being *itself* would not be *good.* Thus, therefore, *if* in some *way they were not* from the First Good and nevertheless in themselves[20] they were *good,* it would follow that in them it would *not* be *the same* that they be of some sort[21] and *that* they be *good, but it would be other* for *them to be and to be* good.

{90} Then when he says: *But if <they were> nothing else at all,* etc., he proves what he had supposed, namely, that in the light of the aforesaid supposition, in them to be good would be one thing, and to be without qualification or to be anything else, another. For *if nothing else at all* were in them *except* that they are *good,* so that, namely, they were *neither heavy nor colored nor distinct*[22] by any *spatial dimension,* as is the case with all bodies, *nor were there any quality in them except* this only, that *they were good; then* it would *not* seem that they were created *things,* but rather that they were the First *Principle* {100} *of things* Itself. For that which is the very Essence of Goodness is the First Principle of things. As a consequence it would not need to be said in the plural of all those that they *would seem* to be the Principle of things, *but rather* in the singular, that *It would seem* to be the First Principle of things, as if all good things would be simply One. For *One alone is,* which is *of this sort,* that It be *only Good* and *nothing else.* This <that all good things be one>, however, is clearly false, and so too is the first <consequent>, namely, that created things, the First Good removed, would be {110} nothing other than This-Which-is-to-be-Good.

Then when he says: *Because they are not,* etc., he shows what judgment about the goodness of things must be made in accord with the truth. And he says that because created things do not possess simplicity in every respect, namely, so that there be in them nothing other than the essence of goodness, they could *not be at all* among the things of na-

scilicet est ipsa essencia bonitatis, sequitur quod quia *esse* rerum creatarum effluxit {120} *a uoluntate* illius qui est essencialiter bonum, ideo res create *bone esse dicuntur. Primum enim bonum,* scilicet Deus, *in eo quod est, bonum est,* quia est essencialiter ipsa bonitas; set *secundum bonum* quod est creatum *est bonum* secundum quod *fluxit* a primo bono quod est per essenciam bonum. Cum igitur *ipsum esse omnium rerum fluxit* a primo bono, consequens est quod *ipsum esse* rerum creatarum sit *bonum,* et quod unaqueque res creata in quantum est sit bona; set sic solum res create *non essent bone* {130} *in eo quod sunt,* si esse earum non procederet *a summo bono.*

Redit ergo eius solutio ad hoc quod esse primi est secundum propriam rationem bonum, quia natura et essencia primi boni nichil aliud est quam bonitas; esse autem secundi boni est quidem bonum, non secundum rationem proprie essencie quia essencia eius non est ipsa bonitas, set uel humanitas uel aliquid aliud huiusmodi, set esse eius habet quod sit bonum ex habitudine ad {140} primum bonum quod est eius causa, ad quod quidem comparatur sicut ad primum principium et ad ultimum finem per modum quo aliquid dicitur sanum quo aliquid ordinatur ad finem sanitatis et dicitur medicinale secundum quod est a principio effectiuo artis medicine. Est igitur considerandum secundum premissa quod in bonis creatis est duplex bonitas, una quidem secundum quod dicuntur bona per relationem ad primum bonum, et secundum hoc et esse eorum et quicquid {150} in eis est a primo bono est bonum; alia uero bonitas consideratur in eis absolute, prout scilicet unumquodque dicitur bonum in quantum est perfectum in esse et in operari, et hec quidem perfectio non competit bonis creatis secundum ipsum esse essenciale eorum, set secundum aliquid superadditum quod dicitur uirtus eorum ut supra dictum est; et secundum hoc ipsum esse eorum non est bonum, set primum horum habet omnimodam perfectionem in ipso suo esse, et ideo {160} esse eius est secundum se et absolute bonum.

ture *unless He had willed them to be:* God, Who is *That Which alone is Good,* inasmuch, namely, as He is the very Essence of Goodness. It follows that because the *being* of created things flows out {120} *from the will* of Him Who is essentially Good, created things *are said to be good.* For the First *Good,* namely God, *is Good in this, that He is,* because He is essentially Goodness Itself. But a *second good,* which is created, *is good* inasmuch as *it has flowed* from the First Good, which is Good through Essence. Therefore, since *the very being of all things has flowed* from the First Good, it follows that the *very being* of created things is *good,* and that each created thing is good inasmuch as it is, but only in this way: that created things *would not be good* {130} *insofar as they are* if their being did not proceed *from the Highest Good.*

His solution comes back to this, therefore, that the Being of the First is good according to Its own intelligible structure because the Nature and Essence of the First Good is nothing other than Goodness. The being of a secondary good is good indeed,[23] not according to the intelligible structure of its own essence—because its essence is not Goodness Itself, but is either humanity or something else of this sort—but its own being possesses this, that it is good owing to a relation to {140} the First Good, which is its Cause, to which it is related as to First Principle and Last End. In this way something is said to be 'healthy,' because by it a thing is ordered to the end of health, and something is termed 'medicinal,' inasmuch as it is from an effective principle of the art of medicine. In accord with the aforesaid, it must be considered that there is a twofold goodness in created goods. One, inasmuch as they are termed 'good' through a relation to the First Good; according to this, both their being, and whatever {150} is in them from the First Good, is good. The other goodness is considered in them absolutely, inasmuch, namely, as each one is termed 'good' insofar as it is complete in being and in operating. And this completion does not belong to created goods according to their essential 'to be'[24] itself, but according to something superadded called their 'virtue,' as was stated above. And according to this, their being itself is not good, whereas the First of them has every sort of completion in Its own Being Itself, and therefore {160} His Being is Good both according to Itself and absolutely.

Qua in re soluta est questio. Idcirco enim, licet in eo quod sint bona sint, non sunt tamen similia primo bono quoniam non quoquo modo sint res ipsum esse earum bonum est. Set quoniam non potest esse ipsum esse rerum nisi a primo esse defluxerit id est bono, idcirco ipsum esse bonum est nec est simile ei a quo est. Illud enim quoquo modo sit bonum est in eo quod est. Non enim aliud est preter quam bonum. Hoc autem nisi ab illo esset bonum fortasse esse posset, set bonum {10} in eo quod est esse non posset. Tunc enim participaret forsitan bono; ipsum uero esse quod non haberent a bono bonum habere non possent.

Igitur sublato ab hiis bono primo mente et cogitatione, ista licet essent bona, tamen in eo quod essent bona esse non possent. Et quoniam actu non potuere existere nisi illud ea quod uere bonum est produxisset, idcirco et esse eorum bonum est et non est simile substanciali bono id quod ab eo fluxit. Et nisi ab eo fluxissent licet essent bona, tamen in eo quod sunt bona {20} esse non possent quoniam et preter bonum et non ex bono essent cum illud ipsum bonum primum est et ipsum esse sit et ipsum bonum et ipsum esse bonum.

At non etiam alba in eo quod sunt alba esse oportebit ea que alba sunt quoniam ex uoluntate Dei fluxerunt ut essent alba? Minime: aliud enim est esse, aliud albis esse. Hoc ideo quoniam qui ea ut essent effecit bonus quidem est, minime uero albus. Voluntatem igitur boni comitatum est ut essent bona in eo quod sunt; uoluntatem uero non albi non est comitata talis {30} ei quidem proprietas ut esset album in eo quod est; neque enim ex albi uoluntate defluxerunt. Itaque, quia uoluit esse ea alba qui erat non albus, sunt alba tantum. Quia uero uoluit ea esse bona qui erat bonus, sunt bona in eo quod sunt.

Secundum hanc igitur rationem, cuncta oportet esse iusta quoniam ipse iustus est qui ea esse uoluit? Ne hoc quidem, nam bonum esse essenciam, iustum uero esse actum respicit. Idem autem est in eo esse quod agere. Idem igitur bonum esse quod iustum. Nobis {40} uero non est idem esse quod agere: non enim

CHAPTER 5

In this very point the question has been solved. For on this account, although they <secondary goods> may be good in this, that they are, still they are not similar to the First Good, because their very being is not good in whatever way things may be. But since the very being of things cannot be unless it flow down from the First Being, that is, from the Good, on that account their very being is good, but is not like That from Which it is. For It, in every way that It is, is Good in this, that It is. For It is nothing other than Good. However, unless this <the secondary good> were from It, perhaps it could be good, but it could not be good {10} in this, that it is. Perhaps it might then participate in good, but its very being, which it[25] *would not possess from the Good, it could not possess as good.*

Therefore, the First Good taken away in mind and thought from these <secondary goods>, although they might be good, still they could not be good in this, that they are. And since they could not actually exist unless That Which is truly Good had produced them, on that account both their being is good and that which flowed from the Substantial Good is not like It. And unless they had flowed from It, although they might be good, still they could not be {20} good in this, that they are, because they would be both outside the Good and not from the Good, whereas that First Good Itself is[26] *Being Itself; and the Good Itself; and Being, the Good Itself.*

But must it not also be the case that white things are white in this, that they are, since they are white because they have flowed from God's will that they be white? Not at all: For it is one thing to be, and another for them to be white. This is the case, therefore, because He who effected that they be, indeed is Good, but surely is not white. Therefore, that they be good in this, that they are, is what accompanied the will of the Good; a property of this sort, that they be white in this, that they are, {30} did not accompany the will of One <Who is> not white; neither have they flowed down from the will of one <who is> white. And so it is that One Who was not white willed them to be white; because of this, are they merely white. Since, however, He Who was Good willed them to be good, they are good in this, that they are.

According to this argument, therefore, is it necessary that all things be just, since He is Just who willed them to be? Neither is this the case, for to be good pertains to essence, whereas to be just pertains to an act. In Him, however, to be is identical with to act; hence <in Him>, to be Good is identical with to be Just.

51

simplices sumus. Non est igitur nobis idem bonis esse quod iustis, set idem nobis est esse omnibus in eo quod sumus; bona igitur omnia sumus, non etiam iusta.

Amplius bonum quidem generale est, iustum uero speciale, nec species desicendit in omnia; idcirco alia quidem iusta, alia aliud, omnia bona.

EXPOSITIO

Qua in re soluta est questio etc.

Postquam determinauit ueritatem premisse questionis, hic soluit obiectionem ex qua concludebatur quod si bona creata sunt bona in eo quod sunt, quod sint similia primo bono, et circa hoc duo facit: primo soluit obiectionem, secundo colligit que dicta sunt, ibi: *Igitur sublato* etc.

Dicit ergo primo quod ex premissis patet hanc questionem esse solutam. Ideo *enim non sunt similia* {10} *primo bono* per *hoc quod* sunt *bona in eo quod* sunt, quia *ipsum esse* rerum creatarum *non est bonum* absolute quocumque *modo* se habeat, set solum secundum habitudinem ad primum bonum; set quia *ipsum esse rerum creatarum non potest esse nisi* deriuetur *a primo* bono, *idcirco ipsum* eorum *esse bonum est nec* tamen *est simile* in bonitate primo bono, quia *illud* absolute est bonum quomodocumque se habeat, quia nichil est in eo aliud nisi ipsa essencia bonitatis. Et hoc ideo est, quia non {20} est in eo perfectio per additionem, set in suo simplici esse habet omnimodam perfectionem ut dictum est. Set bonum creatum forsitan *posset esse bonum* etiam in se consideratum, etiam si detur per impossibile quod non procederet a primo bono, scilicet bonitate que sibi competit absolute, set sic non esset bonum in eo quod est, quia *tunc* esset bonum per participationem bonitatis superaddite, set *ipsum esse* eius non esset bonum, si a bono non deriuaretur; ex huiusmodi habitudine ipsum {30} esse rerum creatarum est bonum.

With us, {40} however, to be is not identical with to act, for we are not simple. To be good, therefore, with us is not identical with to be just, but to be in this, that we are, is identical in all of us; we are all of us, therefore, good things, but not also just.

Furthermore, good is general indeed, whereas just is special, nor does a special class descend to all; on this account, some things indeed are just, others something else, <but> all things are good.

EXPOSITION

In this very point the question has been solved etc.

After he has determined the truth of the aforesaid question, he here solves the objection from which it was concluded that, if created goods are good in this, that they are, they must be similar to the First Good, and with regard to this he does two things. First, he solves the objection; second, he pulls together what had been said, where he says: *Therefore . . . taken away*, etc.

He says first, then, that it is clear from what has gone before that this question has been solved. Therefore, *still they are not similar {10} to the First Good* in *this* manner, *that* they are *good in this, that* they are, because *the very being* of created things *is not good* absolutely in whatever *way* it might be, but only in accord with a relation to the First Good. But because *the very being of created things cannot be unless* derived *from the First* Good, *therefore* their *very being is good*. Nevertheless, <it> *is not like* in goodness to the First Good, since *That* is Good absolutely in whatever way It may stand, because there is nothing in It other than the very Essence of Goodness. And this is so because {20} there is in It no perfection through addition, but in Its Simple Being It possesses every sort of perfection, as has been said. But a created good, even considered in itself, perhaps also *could be good,* namely, by the goodness which belongs to it absolutely, even if it were granted through an impossible stipulation that it would not proceed from the First Good. But thus it would not be good in this, that it is, because *then* <by its goodness belonging absolutely> it would be good through participation in a superadded goodness, but its *very being* would not be good if it were not derived from the Good. From a relationship of this sort the very {30} being of created realities is good.

Deinde cum dicit: *Igitur sublato* etc., colligit in unum que dicta sunt, et dicit quod, si a rebus per intellectum remoueatur primum bonum, omnia alia, *licet* detur quod *essent bona, non tamen* possunt *esse bona in eo quod sunt,* set quia non poterunt esse in *actu nisi* in quantum sunt producta a primo *quod est uere bonum,* ideo etiam esse eorum est bonum. Et tamen esse fluens a bono *non est simile* primo quod est substancialiter bonum, a quo *nisi* omnia {40} *fluxissent, licet essent bona, non* tamen essent bona in eo quod sunt, in quantum scilicet non essent ex primo bono, *cum* tamen *ipsum primum bonum* sit *et ipsum esse,* quia eius esse est sua substancia, *et ipsum bonum,* quia est ipsa essencia bonitatis, *et ipsum esse bonum,* quia in eo non differt esse et quod est.

Deinde cum dicit: *At non etiam* etc., mouet duas obiectiones contra predicta quarum secundam ponit ibi: *Secundum hanc igitur* etc.

{50} Circa primum ponit talem obiectionem. Dictum est quod omnia in eo quod sunt bona sunt, quia ex uoluntate primi boni processit ut essent bona. Nunquid ergo omnia *alba in eo quod sunt alba* sunt, quia *ex uoluntate Dei* processit *ut alba essent?* Set ipse respondet quod *minime* hoc oportet, quia hiis que sunt *alba aliud est esse* simpliciter quod competit eis secundum principia essencialia, et *aliud* est ex quo sunt alba. Et huiusmodi differencie inter album et bonum ratio est quia Deus, qui fecit {60} creata et bona et alba, est *quidem bonus,* non est autem *albus.* Sic *igitur* ad *uoluntatem* primi *boni* consecutum est ut creata *essent bona* in quantum uoluit ea esse bona, et quod *essent bona in eo quod sunt* in quantum sunt a bono producta, quia esse rerum creatarum, ex hoc ipso quod est a bono, habet rationem boni ut dictum est; set *uoluntatem* Dei non est consecuta *talis proprietas* ut id quod est creatum *in eo quod est <esset album>,* propter hoc quod non defluxerit *ex uoluntate albi,* sicut {70} bona *defluxerunt* a uoluntate boni, ut posset dici quod esse eorum est album in quantum sunt a primo albo. Sic igitur manifestum est quod quia Deus qui non est albus *uoluit* aliqua *esse alba,* potest quidem hoc solum dici de eis quod *sunt alba,* non autem quod sunt alba in eo quod sunt. Set quia Deus *qui* est *bonus* uoluit omnia *esse bona,* ideo *sunt bona in eo quod sunt,* in quantum scilicet esse eorum habet rationem boni propter hoc quod est a bono.

Then when he says: *Therefore . . . taken away,* etc., he draws into a unity the things which have been said, and states that if the First Good be
removed from things through the intellect, all other things, *although* it
be granted that *they might be good, still they* could *not be good in this, that
they are.* But since they could not be in *actuality unless* <and> inasmuch
as they are led forth from the First Good *Which is truly Good,* therefore,
too, is their being good. And, nevertheless, being flowing from the Good
is not like the First Which is substantially Good, and from Which *unless*
all {40} *had flowed, although they might be good,* they would *not* be good insofar as they are, inasmuch as they would not be from the First Good.
Whereas, however, the *First Good Itself* is *Being Itself,* because Its To Be is
Its Substance, *and Good Itself,* because It is the very Essence of Goodness,
and Being, the Good Itself, because in It To Be and What It Is do not differ.

Then when he says: *But . . . not also,* etc., he proffers two objections
against what has been already stated, the second of which he sets down
in the place where he says: *According to this . . . therefore,* etc.

{50} The first objection is of this sort. It was stated that all things are
good in this, that they are, because they proceed from the will of the
First Good that they be good. Is it not the case, therefore, that all *white
things* are *white in this, that they are,* because *that they be white* proceeds
from God's will? But he answers that this is *not at all* necessary, since for
those things which are *white it is one thing to be* without qualification,
which belongs to them according to their essential principles, and it is
from *another* <principle> that they are white. And the reason for a difference of this sort between white and good is because God, Who has
made {60} created things both good and white, is *indeed Good,* and yet
He is not *white.* Thus, *therefore,* it follows on the *will* of the First *Good* that
created things *be good* inasmuch as He has willed them to be good, and
that *they be good in this, that they are,* inasmuch as they are produced by
the Good. For the being of created things, from the fact that it is from
the Good, has the character of good, as has been said. But *a property of
this sort,* that what is created <*be white*> *in this, that it is,* is not consequent
upon the *will* of God, for this reason: It did not flow down *from the will of
one white,* in the way that {70} goods *have flowed down* from the will of
the Good, so that it might be said that their being is white inasmuch as
they are from a First White![27] Thus, therefore, it is clear that because
God Who is not white *willed* some things *to be white,* it can, indeed, be

{80} Deinde cum dicit: *Secundum hanc igitur rationem est* etc., ponit secundam obiectionem. Posset enim aliquis dicere: omnia sunt bona in eo quod sunt, quia ille qui est bonus uoluit ea esse bona; pari ratione omnia *oportet esse iusta,* quia ille qui est *iustus uoluit ea esse.* Set ipse respondet quod *hoc* non sequitur duplici ratione. Primo *quidem* quia hoc quod est *bonum* significat naturam quandam siue *essenciam.* Dictum est enim quod Deus est ipsa essencia bonitatis, et unaqueque res secundum {90} perfectionem proprie nature dicitur bona, set iustum dicitur per respectum ad *actum* sicut et quelibet uirtus. *In* Deo *autem idem est esse quod agere,* unde in ipso *idem* est *bonum esse quod iustum* esse; set *nobis non est idem esse quod agere* quia deficimus a simplicitate Dei, unde *nobis non est idem esse* bonos et iustos, *set esse* conuenit *nobis omnibus* in quantum *sumus,* et ideo etiam bonitas omnibus nobis conuenit; set actus quem respicit iusticia non conuenit omnibus, nec in hiis quibus conuenit est idem quod {100} esse ipsorum; unde relinquitur quod *non* omnia sunt iusta in eo quod sunt.

Secundam rationem ponit ibi: *Amplius bonum quidem* etc. Bonum enim *est* quiddam *generale* cuius *quedam* species est iusticia sicut et cetere uirtutes. In Deo autem inuenitur omnis ratio bonitatis, et ideo non solum est bonus set iustus. Non autem omnes species bonitatis inueniuntur in omnibus set diuerse in diuersis, et ideo non oportet quod species que est iusticia deriuetur ad *omnia* encia {110} sicut deriuatur bonitas, unde encium quedam sunt *iusta,* quedam uero habent aliam speciem bonitatis, et tamen *omnia* sunt *bona* in quantum deriuantur a primo bono.

Et in hoc terminatur expositio huius libri. Benedictus Deus per omnia. Amen.

said of them only that *they are white;* not, however, that they are white in this, that they are. But because God *Who* is *Good* has willed all things *to be good,* therefore *they are good in this, that they are,* namely, inasmuch as their being has the character of good because it is from the Good.

{80} Then when he says: *According to this argument therefore, is,* etc., he sets down a second objection. For someone could say: All things are good in this, that they are, because He Who is Good willed them to be good; for a like reason *it is necessary that* all things *be just,* because He Who is *Just willed them to be.* But he answers that *this* does not follow, for two reasons. First, *indeed,* because this term *'good'*[28] signifies a certain nature or *essence.* For it was stated that God is the very Essence of Goodness, and each reality is termed 'good' in accord with {90} the completion of its own nature, but it is called 'just' with respect to an *act,* as is the case with any virtue you like. *In* God, *however, to be is identical with to act;* hence in Him *to be Good* is *identical with* to be *Just.* But *with us* . . . *to be is not identical with to act,* because we fall short of the simplicity of God. Hence, *with us* to be good and to be just *is*[29] *not identical, but to be* belongs *to all of us* inasmuch as *we are,* and therefore goodness, too, belongs to us all. But the act with which justice is concerned does not belong to all; nor, even in those to whom it does belong, is it identical with {100} their being. Hence it remains that *not* all things are just insofar as they are.

He sets down the second reason where he says: *Furthermore, good . . . indeed,* etc. For good *is* something *general* of which *a certain* special class is justice, as is the case with the other virtues. In God, however, every aspect of goodness is to be found, and therefore He is not only Good, but Just. Not all species of goodness, however, are found in all beings, but different ones are in different beings. And therefore it is not necessary that the species that is justice should flow down to *all* beings, {110} as goodness flows down. Hence, some beings are *just,* whereas some have another species of goodness, and yet *all* are *good* inasmuch as they are derived from the First Good.

And in this the exposition of this book comes to an end. Blessed be God in everything! Amen.

NOTES TO THE TRANSLATION

1. The phrase *in eo quod sunt* (singular, *in eo quod est;* here, *in eo quod sint*) we translate both as "in this, that they are" and as "insofar as they are". The first translation is very literal and is preferred by us. The Latin phrase itself could also be translated as "in that which they are"; however, to use this translation consistently would lead to problems in the interpretation of Boethius. As is clear from the treatise, he claims that creatures are good *in eo quod sunt* because they are from God: This could mean that they are good in what they are because they are from God, as well as that they are good just insofar as they are, inasmuch as they exist, because they are from God. Now in L.2.B10–15 Boethius contrasts being something, i.e., being in some respect, such as white, with being something *in eo quod est*, which in context signifies being without qualification, simply being. One can conclude from the rest of the treatise, for example, from L.3.B14–20, L.4.B11–25, and L.5.B1–20, that according to Boethius for creatures to be is the same as to be good, only because they are from God. This kind of "to be" is the non-accidental kind, and thus is associated with being *in eo quod sunt*. But it would be a problem for Boethius to say that for a creature to be good is the same as for it to be in that which it is (if speaking this way makes any sense at all), for that would seem to imply that for the creature to be good is the same as for it to be *what* it is, which would imply that the creature is God.

We do interpret Boethius as saying that the essence of a creature is good because it is from God, and for this reason the creature is good insofar as it is (or, "in this, that it is"). But the identity in the creature is between its actually existing and its being good, not between its essence and goodness. Its essence is good, but is not goodness. This does not mean that Boethius posits an act of being as a distinct metaphysical principle, as Aquinas does. As has been explained, in his mature works Aquinas identifies the goodness of a creature with its *esse,* or act of being—a principle distinct from its essence. Of course, the translation we choose for *in eo quod sunt* does accommodate Aquinas's emphasis on *esse* as the act of being and principle of goodness.

2. Another, and more common, translation is "You also say this ought to be done because the method of writings of this sort is not known to all." Our translation comports with Aquinas's interpretation of this passage in L.1.A78–83. Here Aquinas says that Boethius first shows that he intends to speak obscurely, and second shows that this was a customary manner for him, where he says, "Still . . . the ekdomads" *(Ekdomadas vero).* Aquinas elaborates in L.1.A85–117; he also says here that John himself had requested obscure treatment.

3. We avoid "essence" or "nature," as a translation of *ratio,* for the most part using "intelligible structure" or "character"; on occasion we use "aspect" or "notion." In the Introduction we defend the position that Boethius uses *esse* in the

sense of "essence"; our use of "essence" or "nature," then, must be very precise, and so we employ these terms only to translate the equivalent Latin *essencia* and *natura*. Indeed, in some passages Aquinas uses all three terms—i.e., *ratio, essencia,* and *natura*—and even speaks of the *ratio* of an essence (L.4.A136) and the *ratio* of an essential nature (L.2.A305); these terms must, then, be distinguished. For considerations of precision we also restrict our use of "definition" to those passages in which Aquinas uses *diffinitio.*

4. Note that although Boethius uses *esse,* Aquinas uses *ens* here.

5. Boethius does not speak of an act of being, *actus essendi,* but the form of being, *forma essendi.*

6. Aquinas is quoting Boethius but substitutes *ens* for *id quod est,* and uses *esse* to mean "to be," the act of being.

7. That is, it will be said to be simply, or without qualification, owing to its substantial act of "to be."

8. In this translated formula we have changed the order used previously, so as to reflect the order of Aquinas's commentary at this point.

9. Here, and in (175–78) below, Aquinas seems to be appealing to the double meaning of *in eo quod est:* See note 1 above.

10. To accommodate the flow of Aquinas's commentary we here translate *omni compositio aliud est . . . aliud* differently from the way we did in L.2.B17.

Note that Boethius does not use the terminology "to be *a being*"; Aquinas, according to the Leonine editors, adds *ens,* which makes the formulation somewhat puzzling. But it is possible that Aquinas did not add the *ens.* As John F. Wippel indicates in *The Metaphysical Thought of Thomas Aquinas: From Finite Being to Uncreated Being* (Washington, D.C.: The Catholic University of America Press, 2000), p. 162, n.80, the manuscripts do not unanimously support inclusion of *ens;* indeed, Wippel suggests that there is "philosophical and contextual" evidence for its exclusion. If it is excluded, the English translation should be: "and so he says that in *every* composite *it is one thing* to be, and *another* to be the composite itself, which IS by participating in *being itself.*"

11. Here Aquinas is speaking of forms that are simple only in that they lack matter, as is clear from the above.

12. Literally, "that which they are are good: *id quod sunt bona sunt.*"

13. "Very being" translates *ipsum esse,* which is also translated sometimes as "being itself."

14. *Nicomachean Ethics* 1.1; 1094a2.

15. Of course, although for Aristotle animality exists only in individuals, it exists in animals other than humans.

16. Literally, "in the definition of that about which it is said": *in diffinitione eius de quo dicitur.*

17. *In eo quod ipsum est* in the Boethian text above (L.3.B8–9) we translate "insofar as it itself is." Again, the two meanings discussed in note 1 above come into play here.

18. Here Aquinas is speaking of something's receiving the act of being; hence, our use of "to be."

19. *Nicomachean Ethics,* 2.6; 1106a15–17.

20. *In se,* "in themselves," is not in the text of Boethius.

21. *Talia,* "of some sort," is not in the text of Boethius.

22. *Distincta;* in Boethius the term is *distenta.* The Leonine editors express some doubt about the use of "distincta" in Aquinas: vol. 50. p. 278, note to Boethius l. 27.

23. According to Aquinas, however, *esse* as the act of being is the "to be good"; *esse* is not simply "good."

24. That is, their substantial act of being, or "to be."

25. Boethius uses the plural here; we keep the singular in this sentence for consistency.

26. We ignore the "est," as does Tester. Aquinas himself does not take it into account: L.5.A43–46.

27. That is, it cannot be said that creatures are white inasmuch as they are from a First White, because they are *not* from a First White: God is not white, although God is the Good.

28. Literally, "because this that is good": *quia hoc quod est bonum.*

29. Of course good English would require "are" instead of "is," but the latter reflects the Latin of Aquinas and Boethius.

SELECT BIBLIOGRAPHY

Ancient and Medieval Authors

Alan of Lille. *Regulae Alani de sacra theologia.* PL 210 621–684.

Aristotle. *Aristoteles latinus,* XXV 3.2, *Metaphysica,* Lib. I–XIV, Recensio et Translatio Guillelmi de Moerbeka, ed. G. Vuillemin-Diem. Leiden, New York, Cologne: E.J. Brill, 1995.

Augustine, Saint. *Confessionum tredecim libri,* ed. M. Skutella, L. Verheijen, CCSL 27. Turnhout: Brepols, 1981. PL 32 659–868.

———. *Contra Academicos libri tres,* ed. W.m. Green, CCSL 29, pp. 3–61. Turnhout: Brepols, 1970. PL 32 905–958.

———. *De ciuitate dei,* ed. B. Dombart, A. Kalb, CCSL 47, 48. Turnhout: Brepols, 1955. PL 41 13–804.

———. *De diversis quaestionibus LXXXIII liber unus,* ed. A. Mutzenbecher, CCSL 44 A, pp. 11–249. Turnhout: Brepols, 1975. PL 40 11–100.

———. *De libero arbitrio libri tres,* ed. W.M. Green, CSEL 74, pp. 3–154. Vienna: Hoelder-Pichler-Tempsky, 1956; PL 32 1221–1310.

———. *De natura boni,;* ed. J. Zycha, CSEL 25, section 6, part 2, pp. 853–889. Prague: F. Tempsky; Vienna: F. Tempsky; Leipzig: G. Freytag, 1892. PL 42 551–572.

———. *De Trinitate,* ed. W.J. Mountain, CCSL 50, 50A. Turnhout: Brepols, 1968. PL 42 819–1098.

Avicenna. *Avicenna latinus. Liber de Philosophia prima sive Scientia divina, I–IV,* series *Avicenna latinus,* ed. S. Van Riet, Introduction by G. Verbeke. Louvain: E. Peeters; Leiden: E.J. Brill, 1977.

———. *Liber de Philosophia prima sive Scientia divina, V–X.* Louvain: E. Peeters; Leiden: E.J. Brill, 1980.

———. *Liber de Philosophia prima sive Scientia divina, Lexiques,* by S. Van Riet. Louvain-la-neuve. E. Peeters; Leiden: E.J. Brill, 1983.

Boethius. *De arithmetica.* PL 63 1079–1168.

———. *In Categorias Aristotelis libri quattuor,* ed. 2. PL 64 159–294.

———. *Boethius's In Ciceronis Topica,* tr. Eleonore Stump. Ithaca and London: Cornell University Press, 1988. PL 64 1039–1169.

———. *In Eisagogen Porphyrii commenta,* ed. G. Schepss, S. Brandt. CSEL 48, Editio prima, pp. 3–132, Editio secunda, pp. 133–348. Vienna: F. Tempsky, Leipzig: G. Freytag, 1906. PL 64, Editio prima, pp. 9–48, Editio secunda, pp. 47–158.

———. *Liber De interpretatione.* PL 64, Editio prima, pp. 293–392, Editio secunda, pp. 393–640.

———. *The Theological Tractates. The Consolation of Philosophy,* tr. H.F. Stewart, E.K.

Rand, S.J. Tester. The Loeb Classical Library. Cambridge, Mass., and London: Harvard University Press, new ed. 1973; rpt. 1990.

———. *Boethius's De topicis differentiis*, tr. Eleonore Stump. Ithaca and London: Cornell University Press, 1978. PL 64 1173–1216.

Cassiodorus, *Variarum, Monumenta Germaniae Historiae*, Auctores antiquissimi, vol. 12. Berlin: Weidmann, 1894.

Cicero, Marcus Tullius. *De divinatione*, in *Cicero in Twenty-eight Volumes, XX*, tr. William A. Falconer. The Loeb Classical Library. Cambridge: Harvard University Press; London: W. Heinemann Ltd., 1923–1979.

———. *De finibus*, in *Cicero in Twenty-eight Volumes, XVII*, tr. H. Rackham. The Loeb Classical Library. Cambridge: Harvard University Press; London: W. Heinemann, 1914–71.

———. *M. Tulli Ciceronis opera quae supersunt omnia*, ed. J.G. Baiter, C.L. Kayser. Leipzig: Tauchnitz, 1869

Clarembald of Arras. *Life and Works of Clarembald of Arras, A Twelfth-Century Master of the School of Chartres*, ed. Nikolaus M. Häring. Studies and Texts 10. Toronto: Pontifical Institute of Mediaeval Studies, 1965.

Gilbert of Poitiers. *The Commentaries on Boethius by Gilbert of Poitiers*, ed. Nikolaus M. Häring. Studies and Texts 13. Toronto: Pontifical Institute of Mediaeval Studies, 1966.

Proclus. *The Elements of Theology*, tr. E.R. Dodds, 2d ed. Oxford: Clarendon Press, 1933; rpt. 1971.

Thierry of Chartres. *Commentaries on Boethius by Thierry of Chartres and His School*, ed. Nikolaus M. Häring. Studies and Texts 20. Toronto: Pontifical Institute of Mediaeval Studies, 1971.

Thomas Aquinas, *Sancti Thomae de Aquino Opera omnia*, Tomus 50; *Super Boetium De trinitate*, ed. P.-M.J. Gils, pp. 75–171; *Expositio libri Boetii De ebdomadibus*, ed. L.-J. Bataillon, C.A. Grassi, pp. 267–82. Rome: Commissio Leonina, Paris: Éditions du cerf, 1992.

———. *Thomas Aquinas. On Being and Essence*, tr. Armand Maurer, 2d revised edition. Toronto: Pontifical Institute of Mediaeval Studies, 1968.

———. *Faith, Reason and Theology*, Questions I–IV of his Commentary on the *De Trinitate* of Boethius, tr. Armand Maurer. Mediaeval Sources in Translation 32. Toronto: Pontifical Institute of Mediaeval Studies, 1987.

———. *Scriptum super libros Sententiarum Magistri Petri Lombardi Episcopi Parisiensis*. 4 vols.: vols. 1 and 2 ed. R.P. Mandonnet; vols. 3 and 4 ed. M.F. Moos. Paris: Lethielleux, 1929–1947. Vol. 4 ends at Liber 4, Distinctio 22, Quaestio 2; for Distinctiones 23–50 see *Opera omnia sancti Thomae Aquinatis*, vol. 11. Paris: Vivès, 1874.

———. *Summa contra gentiles* (Leonine manual edition). Rome: Leonine Commission, 1934.

———. *Summa theologiae* (text of Pius V with Leonine variants), 5 vols. Ottawa: Commissio Piana, 1941.

Valla, Laurentius. *Opera omnia*, 2 vols. Basel: Henricus Petrus, 1540, rpt. Turin: Bottega d'Erasmo, 1962. [Monumenta Politica et Philosophica Rariora, ex op-

timis editionibus phototypice expressa, curante Luigi Firpo, series 1, numerus 6.]

William of Auvergne, *William of Auvergne. De trinitate,* ed. Bruno Switalski. Studies and Texts 34. Toronto: Pontifical Institute of Mediaeval Studies, 1976.

Modern Authors

Chadwick, Henry. *Boethius. The Consolations of Music, Logic, Theology, and Philosophy.* Oxford: The Clarendon Press, 1981.

Collins, James. "Progress and Problems in the Reassessment of Boethius." *The Modern Schoolman* 23.1 (November 1945), pp. 1–23.

Courcelle, Pierre. *Recherches sur les "Confessions" de s. Augustin.* Paris: de Boccard, 1950.

De Rijk, L.M. "On Boethius's Notion of Being." In *Meaning and Inference in Mediaeval Philosophy: Studies in Memory of Jan Pinborg,* ed. Norman Kretzmann, pp. 1–29. Synthese Historical Library, vol. 32. Dordrecht/Boston/London: Kluwer Academic Publishers, 1988.

Duhem, Pierre. *Le système du monde.* 5 vols. Paris: Hermann, 1917.

Fay, Charles. "Boethius' Theory of Goodness and Being." In *Readings in Ancient and Mediaeval Philosophy,* ed. James Collins, pp. 164–72. Westminster, Md.: Newman Press, 1960.

Gibbon, Edward. *The History of the Decline and Fall of the Roman Empire,* ed. J.B. Bury. 7 vols. London: Methuen, 1909–1914.

McDonald, Scott. "Boethius's Claim That All Substances Are Good." *Archiv fur Geschichte der Philosophie* 70.3 (1988), pp. 245–79.

McInerny, Ralph. *Boethius and Aquinas.* Washington D.C.: The Catholic University of America Press, 1990.

Pegis, Anton Charles. "The Mind of St. Augustine." *Mediaeval Studies* 6 (1944), pp. 1–61.

Schultz, Janice L. "Thomistic Metaethics and a Present Controversy." *The Thomist* 52.1 (January 1988), pp. 40–62.

———. "Is-Ought: Prescribing and a Present Controversy." *The Thomist* 49.1 (January 1985), pp. 1–23.

Silk, Edmund Taite. "Boethius's *Consolatio Philosophiae* as a Sequel to Augustine's *Dialogues* and *Soliloquia.*" *Harvard Theological Review* 32.1 (1939), pp. 19–39.

Synan, Edward A. "An Augustinian Testimony to Polyphonic Music?" *Musica Disciplina* 18 (1964), pp. 3–6.

———. "Boethius, Valla, and Gibbon." *The Modern Schoolman* 69.3 & 4 (March/May 1992), pp. 475–91.

Wippel, John F. *The Metaphysical Thought of Thomas Aquinas: From Finite Being to Uncreated Being.* Washington, D.C.: The Catholic University of America Press, 2000.

An Exposition of the On the Hebdomads *of Boethius* was composed in Meridien and designed and produced by Kachergis Book Design, Pittsboro, North Carolina, and printed on 60-pound Glatfelter Natural Smooth and bound by Sheridan Books, Ann Arbor, Michigan.